T0113519

YOUR TAROT JOURNEY

SAMANTHA MARIE MERSCHOFF

authorHOUSE®

AuthorHouse™
1663 Liberty Drive
Bloomington, IN 47403
www.authorhouse.com
Phone: 833-262-8899

Published by AuthorHouse 09/02/2020

ISBN: 978-1-7283-7140-5 (sc)
ISBN: 978-1-7283-7321-8 (e)

Print information available on the last page.

This book is printed on acid-free paper.

INTRODUCTION

Have you ever had something call to you? People always ask me about what got me into reading. You could hold a gun to my head, and I wouldn't be able to give you a better reason than "Just because". When I was about 17, I just walked past a Rider Waite deck in a bookstore and brought them home with me. I had always been into the occult and realized the power of my intuition, but I never practiced any kind of Oracle.

You probably study tarot for the exact same reason and may even find yourself naturally gifted. It›s no coincidence that tarot readers often get called to the cards. That›s not to say if you›re having trouble interpreting a spread you are not a good reader - but these kinds of studies will come naturally over many years.

I remember my first reading I tried to do myself. I laid all 78 of the Rider Waite cards on the table to see which one "pulled" to me. I describe the "pull" as just an instinctual knowing. I had used this skill in the past to test my intuition so I knew if tarot reading was something I could channel then this would be the way to do it.

The first card I drew was The Sun and at the time I made the biggest mistake I could as a beginner. I relied too heavily on the source material for the definition of the card. I read the wordy, complicated definition and it made me feel a bit discouraged. I didn't understand why I drew that card at the time but when I did it was certainly an "ah ha!!!" Moment. Even with experience, sometimes the message is blatant and sometimes it can take time to notice the synchronicity.

Thankfully I didn't give up and each day I pulled a card on myself and journaled about it. After about a year or so I didn't care about what the book said. By that point I had developed a relationship with the cards which is the mark of a true reader.

Perspective:

Every reader sees things differently and has a different relationship with their cards. The relationship you will forge with your cards is one of the most sacred and critical bonds you will likely ever forge. Not because it's seemingly a key to understanding the unknown, but tarot is also the key to understanding yourself. Tarot has challenged me in ways that have better prepared me for what my future had in store for me.

With this book, I am hoping to help you build your relationship so you can enjoy these benefits as well.

CHAPTER 1

Tarot Myths and legends

The concept of tarot card reading has been around for centuries mystifying generations of people. Over years its garnered and inspired several myths and legends about the craft that has both scared people away and deemed it sacrilege. There was a time when occult study was punishable by death. Many fabrications and ghost stories were spread to keep people away from the practice.

Tarot card reading is based on a game that was played in Egypt but wasn't used in fortune telling until the renaissance period in Europe. Unfortunately, the world soon engaged in a witch hunt and fortune telling was considered devil work. Tarot card reading returned to the shadows becoming more mythologized than ever before.

Tarot card reading did not meet a massive resurgence until the 19th century. Psychics, mediums, and spirit photography became very popular with the witch trials far behind them. People were finally able to practice publicly without being executed.

Going to a psychic was no more a secret and many

people threw psychic parties and collected Egyptian artifacts. Tarot cards are based heavily on Egyptian lore and trended throughout the United states. Although the spiritual movement was beneficial to some genuinely gifted people, it also attracted several fraudsters. With the use of stage magic and props the people of the 19th century were easily fooled. Eventually many of these fraudsters were exposed by groups including the famous magician Harry Houdini who specialized in illusion. After so many scams and frauds were exposed genuinely, talented psychics were forgotten by history and the campaign against the fraudsters have left a scar on the practice.

Till this day New York state still has a fortune telling ban where psychics (like me) need to make various disclosures before we perform such as what we are doing is for entertainment purposes only. I don't agree with my disclosure but comply to keep my butt out of jail.

Even though the law is forgotten and rarely enforced, less diligent psychics get caught up in mass busts organized by police. Normally when a person has been scammed by a psychic they are too embarrassed to alert authorities so most offenders are taken in groups. Many fraudulent psychics move from town to town changing their names before facing any real consequences.

If you feel an alleged psychic is fishing for information and are trying to scam you out of your money, then you are probably right. Always trust your instincts above all else. These feelings may not feel logical or fair towards others, but they are there to help us protect ourselves.

Unfortunately tarot card reading and other psychic services carry a stigma even though society has become more tolerant of occult practices. Enveloped in a haze of mystery that both scares people away and infatuates those with its magic. This chapter will explore the various myths around tarot cards and debunk several fabrications.

1. You can never buy your own deck, and should only have it gifted.

This common myth has kept many people from pursuing tarot card reading. I'm not even sure where this myth originated from whether it be from Hollywood or other psychics. My best bet is that it was created by psychics to try and stifle anyone from breaking into the business and thus adding on to the mysticism. It could have also been a way for religious fanatics to keep their loved ones away from the craft.

It doesn't matter how you get your first deck. Tarot cards are just cardboard play cards at the end of the day. They have no real power by themselves and you shouldn't ever feel afraid to pick up a deck of cards. You will not face any kind of spiritual backlash. I would recommend buying your own deck because feeling that "call" was the first step in my tarot journey. Out of the 10 decks I own only one of them was gifted to me. As long as you follow your intuition in choosing your deck you can't go wrong.

2. Tarot card reading is satanic by nature.

Thanks to the witch trials tarot reading is closely associated with witches and satanism. There are even strong depictions of the Devil, Angel's and Adam and Eve throughout the Rider Waite deck. However, you do not need to be spiritual to practice tarot. Many witches today use tarot cards even though reading tarot is not a requirement in Wicca.

Tarots association with Satanism stems from people mistakenly linking Wicca to Satanism. Despite having a devil card in the Rider Waite deck that card does not have any biblical meaning.

The devil is a deep card about humanity and our tendency to use scapegoats. In every culture throughout history mankind has blamed wars, natural disasters and even bad behavior on the devil. The lovers are chained to the devil and are feigning helplessness. Looking at the chains you can tell that they are loose and that they can escape at any time. People enjoy playing the victim and this card forces us to be honest with ourselves. As far as any connection to Satan goes it is all a product of superstition and Hollywood.

3. Tarot reading invites bad spirits.

There have been nights where my brother has screamed at me because he believed that my tarot cards attracted a spirit into the house. As a medium it doesn't surprise me that paranormal activity is more noticeable around me. You may even notice an increase in paranormal activity in your own life during your studies. It's not that you are becoming a beacon of weirdness, you are simply becoming more perceptive of what is going on around you.

Exercising your intuition will allow you to receive more

information than you normally would have. Spirits are around you all the time, but you may be overlooking them. Tarot card reading does not increase these happenings but intensifies your connection with the phenomena.

Negative entities are usually attracted by negative thoughts and feelings. Negative thought patterns and actions will make you a target because they see that you are weakened. Just like sharks they can smell blood in the water. They won't attack you if you are strongly swimming through life but will attack those who are struggling. This doesn't mean that you are responsible for bringing a psychic attack on yourself, or for every bad thing that happens to you (especially any kind of abuse). Falling into hard times and feeling down is just part of life and being human. However, being aware of the predatory nature of these negative entities can help you take preventive measures against psychic attack.

Reading tarot exercises your connection to your subconscious and is a good way to take inventory of the energies around you. Although they do not invite energies, they can be helpful in understanding their nature.

4. You always need a fixed spread.

I've seen far too many people begin their tarot journey by trying to remember large spreads like the Tetrakys or the Celtic cross, but you don't really need an elaborate spread to interpret a message. With my style of reading, less is more. There's nothing wrong with using spreads, but spreads are easier once you've built a relationship with your deck. Otherwise you will mistake several placements as contradictory. I feel like larger spreads should be saved for deep introspection and using a maximum of 3 cards to answer smaller questions.

Tarot has virtually no rules and a loose format to begin with, so it never made sense to me to try and contain it in a spread. It's okay if you decide to use larger spreads but just know that you don't have to. Many spreads can be simplified to a 3-card format. I will go over that in an upcoming chapter.

5. There is only one way to interpret a card.

Every card is assigned a general theme whether it be by your love life or career. This kind of thinking seems to complicate readings because there is nothing keeping someone from pulling a Pentacles card in a love reading. Reversals cause even more confusion. It's important to keep an open mind when reading tarot and to allow her to come naturally. Flexible thinking will allow you to interpret quickly. Cards do have General definitions but your personal relationship with each card is much more important.

6. Tarot cards predict death.

A fortune teller foreshadowing someone's death is a common trope in Hollywood. The reader always seems to pull the tower, the devil, x of swords and finally death for dramatic effect. Tarot cards will never predict literal death. Death represents an abrupt unavoidable change. Think of it as the death of your past self that encourages you to let go.

Predicting actual death or even illness in tarot is not only wrong but irresponsible. Never tell your current that they are going to die.

7.Tarot cards have special powers.

Whenever I do in person readings or have my cards out people seem to act nervously around them. I always need to tell them that it's okay to touch them. They are only a piece of cardboard! They only have as much power as you give them like any other Oracle. Relax!!

8.Tarot originates from Egypt.

This is true in a sense that it is loosely based off an old Egyptian card game and the artwork is inspired by ancient Egyptian lore. Historically speaking tarot was not used as divination until the renaissance period in Europe. During the 19th century Egyptian culture became trendy and the tarot cards began adopting Egyptian themes to play on the mystique. Soon people began to believe that the ancient Egyptians invented tarot as they had known it in modern times. Egyptians never used them for divination, but their culture still plays a huge part in the symbolism used.

By the time I publish this book even more myths will have been born. It's impossible to cover all of them but when you study the cards you will begin to have a better head for what is true and false. If you're ever unsure, just try to keep an open mind and do some research! Not everything is always as it seems.

9. Only psychics can use tarot cards.

You don't necessarily need any psychic ability to read tarot cards. You don't even need to be a witch to enjoy tarot cards either. Like Reiki, tarot is not religious or necessarily a spiritual practice. Tarot card reading is a form of divination that works off the subconscious. It has more to do with your relationship with yourself than it does with any deity or God.

10.Tarot was invented by gypsies.

This has been a myth that has existed since the carnival days. However, there's no proof of this being the case. There is no conclusive evidence that tarot reading was created by gypsies. In fact, nobody is quite sure where the origins lie. The popular belief is that it was first used for fortune-telling during the Renaissance. In Europe.

11.Tarot can't be read over the phone.

I would say that at least 60% of the readings I do is over the phone. I've also done several readings over texting, Skype, and messaging. I even perform readings live on Periscope which is a live streaming service. The only things a Tarot reader needs is a sharp intuition and the ability to decipher messages from their deck.

12.Your tarot cards must be kept in silk.

Many people believe tarot cards must be kept in a silk bag when not in use. You can keep your cards anywhere as long as they won't get damaged by water or the sun. The environment won't directly impact the metaphysical properties of the cards. The only thing that will directly impact the cards is the state of your mind. Having a clean calm mind while performing a reading is very important.

13. Reversed cards are always bad.

Nobody likes it when cards like the devil, and deaths are drawn. The death card used to haunt me years ago turning up almost every day. But one day I decided to confront the reason I felt like running away from death and now it's comforting. Death is change that comes for us all and support that we accept it and move on. Now the death card represents my attempts to build a new life.

No card is inherently good or bad because of their kind of patients. The nine of cups is considered one of the most positive cards in the tarot. However, it could also represent wishful thinking in an unhealthy importance of material value. You will feel a pain like sensation in your gut when you are given a warning. Your perceptions of the cards will change as you practice 30 years.

CHAPTER 2

Spreads

When you're first starting out it can be hard to find your way, and therefore so many people use spreads. Sometimes the open-ended nature of tarot reading can be confusing and the structure of a spread helps themes come out strongly. Using a spread can be much easier than just running off pure intuition. It helps place the cards in a more coherent manner.

When I tell people, I can do a reading on anything it's because I've become adept of using spreads over the years. I was once tasked to do a reading to decide whether my querent should get a belly button ring. At first, I was stumped (who the hell gets a reading for this anyway??) But I knew there had to be something I could do. Given that it was a yes or no question I offered to use my pendulum but my querent insisted I use my cards. This happens all the time, and its important to comply to their needs. Pendulum reading may not have resonated with him the same way tarot cards did. I ended up using a 3 card to adapt to the question because yes or no questions are often difficult to interpret. There was no reason to make this reading more complicated than it needed to be. I'll continue this story in another chapter.

This kind of decisions will come more naturally as you develop your style. Throughout this chapter I will go through the basics of spreads and help you find out what method works for you. First and foremost, there are some questions you'll need to answer before you begin....

Why should I do a reading?

Doing a reading is a great way to meditate on issues and find some clarity. Here are some good reasons to do a tarot reading.

1. You feel confused.
2. You feel lost.
3. You would like to learn more about yourself.
4. You need reassurance.
5. You are trying to connect to your spirit guides or your higher self.

All of these are valid reasons for picking up your deck. The more you use your deck the more connected and fluent you will become. You shouldn't run to your deck for everything though.

Early into my tarot journey I made the mistake of relying on my deck for everything. I was hung up on some guy and I really wanted my cards to tell me what I wanted to hear. Your cards will NOT coddle to your insecurities.

There are also several other instances where you should never consult your tarot deck.

When you should NEVER do a reading...

1. You are trying to figure out when you or someone else will die.
2. You are trying to diagnose or gain advice on any medical problem. Always consult a medical professional.
3. You are trying to figure out if you are pregnant.
4. You are using them on gambling. Your deck will play tricks on you and you will most likely lose a lot of money.
5. You are desperately trying to find out how to make someone love you. This is toxic for yourself but is a complete disregard of another person's free will.
6. You have already asked your deck a specific question before. If you continually pull on the same question you will only cause yourself more confusion. Trust your deck and first gut feelings even if it is something you don't want to accept.

Although tarot is a pretty flawless practice all of this is a huge no no as far as readings go. No professional tarot reader should ever try and read in this context. Tarot is too open ended and giving bad advice can not only be dangerous but fatal. If a querent ever comes to you for these purposes it is your responsibility to turn them away and explain to them why it can be harmful to them.

Why should I use a spread?

Jumping onto your first spread can be intimidating as a fledgling reader. You're trying to learn your cards and now you're being asked to define several of them at once in a comprehensive way. But here is a secret - understanding a spread the exact second you look at it is like winning the lottery. Almost every time I do a reading, I must give myself time to digest it. There are even times when I must take a picture of the spread because parts of it just don't make sense at the moment. This is okay. You don't want to rush to conclusions. Take time reading tarot to reflect on the card at play. It will only help you get closer to your answer. Nothing is ever set in stone and Tarot does not offer instant gratification. For this reason, I believe spreads or best using introspection rather than simple yes-or-no questions.

Good examples of questions you can use for a spread...

How can I find love?
What are the factors that are affecting my relationship?
How should I move forward with my career?
What does the new year hold for me?
Spreads are effective with these questions because they allow you to look at all sides of an issue and not just the face value. In my relationship cross I can see the factors affecting both the querent and their partner as well as their past and the current issue in their present. The spread will also show the most likeable outcome at the factors good or bad do not change. The purpose of a spread is to get in-depth answers about a situation without it getting unorganized

and confusing. I'm often asked what kind of readings I do, and I normally tell them I can do a reading on pretty much everything. I almost always do a spread rather than a single card reading on another person to gain more insight. Some readers will soon realize there are spreads they've grown add up to. Although I'm capable of doing hundred spreads I specialize in relationships in matters of the heart. This is a result of having more experienced these spreads as well as my own personal life experiences.

My abilities particularly connect with a person's feelings and subconscious. Although I believe to a certain extent that everyone has psychic ability that we all have our own unique talents and niches. I'm personally adept with addressing trauma and feelings of fear, security, and hopelessness. I suffer from PTSD due to being molested as a child and it brings me feelings of fulfillment when I feel like I can help others with these feelings. Every reader may be different. You may specialize in doing readings on money or different career paths. Some readers are even great at handling 9 card personality spreads. The most basic rule is that you need to be open to reading energy.

If at first, you struggle with spreads remember to be patient with yourself. Nobody becomes an expert overnight. It took me years to get to where I am today, and nobody truly masters the tarot. Tarot is a constant learning experience.

In the next few sections I will share some of my favorite spreads to use. I did not create these nor are they unique to my or anyone else's work. These are as basic and Bare Bones as you get, and they are the first ones I used on my own Journey but before we begin...

How do I know what cards to pull?

Some readers develop their own solid routine pulling cards. I know a psychic that will always have her querent place their hands on our deck and ask a question while cutting cards. Then the psychic will shuffle and pick the cards on the top, bottom, and middle. Personally, I don't have a routine aside from power shuffling before the reading. I only do this to shake off any residual energy or thought forms lingering throughout my deck. After that I just ride on my intuition. Sometimes I feel like I need to shuffle until I feel a pull. Other times I have my querent pull their cards. Sometimes I have an image of a card appear in my head immediately, so I search my deck for it and pull out the surrounding cards. It's okay to have a routine - or not! Practice and you'll find out what works for you.

Whatever you do, never omit a card you pulled or replace it with one that you feel makes more sense. You may need to trust your deck and intuition. You pulled that card for a reason. Removing it will only pollute the energy of the spread and then you will only be seeing what you want to see. This is one of the major rules with using spreads.

With all that, have fun exploring these next few spreads. Good luck with your practice and remember to be patient with yourself. You got this!

YES & NO

I've said this before, but I'll repeat myself for good measure. Yes or no questions are by far my least favorite techniques, but they are not completely useless. They're often difficult because of the in-depth nature of Tarot there's almost never some cookie-cutter answer for big life questions. I normally only use yes or no questions if I'm in a pinch, but it always has been consistent with my intuition anyway. If you'd like the practice or try it out for yourself, here is what I normally do using the Rider Waite deck.

The Rider Waite deck is split into three separate arcanas: Majors, Minors, and Court cards.

At face value a yes answer will either be any major card like The Magician or The World or it will be an even numbered card from the Minor Arcana such as the Two of Cups or Six of Pentacles.

At face value a no card will be a court card like the King of Swords or the Knight of Wands or it will be an odd number card from the Minor Arcana such as the Ace of Pentacles or the Three of Wands.

There are oftentimes the system does not work for me and my intuition and eventual results are not consistent with the structure. Use this method at your own discretion.

PAST, PRESENT, FUTURE

This is easily the most popular and easy to use spread because it's almost impossible to forget. The past present future spread is a simple spread to see where your life is heading and what past events have contributed to it. This is an important spread to get a hang of because it's important in parts of many other spreads.

Past: this card will represent an important event in the parents' life. This event is either hindering the growth or something to channel into to help them push through the next obstacle. For example, the Six of Pentacles will ask you to channel the happiness of your experiences you had as a child

Present: this represents your current state or an upcoming event that will happen very soon. The justice card usually comes pretty loaded with positive and negative attributes regardless of which card it is. For example, the Nine of Cups is generally a positive card and is linked to manifestation. However, it could also be a warning about materialism or wishful thinking.

Future: the most important thing to remember is that your future is subject to change. If you can see an outcome that is negative, then you will find clues on how to change it from the other two cards. If you see something positive, make sure that you are taking appropriate actions to facilitate your success. I could tell you that I see a promotion coming at work, but if you decide to kick up your feet and slack off you may ruin your opportunity. There are certain factors that cannot be changed and that usually pertains to the world around us. For example, if you were to draw Death you will not literally die. It will predict a sudden and uncomfortable change. Looking at the other cards you should have an idea what that is. Remember death is unavoidable and it sucks but it's necessary for change. Your old life will die and begin anew. In this instance it would be a good idea to make sure you don't build your castles in the Sky.

THE WORLD

Remember when I told you that the past, present, future is an important structure and other spreads? The world spread is an adaptation for current life events. The spread is a staple in my readings with other people and really makes me better connect to the querent.

The first thing I do is power shuffle my deck while channeling the querants energy. When I feel the pull the stop, I then search through my deck for the world card. In the spread the world card sheds its definition and only represents you.

1. Recent past - important recent events in the querent past.
2. The world - only a placeholder for the querent. No further definition.
3. Recent future - What will happen next.

RELATIONSHIP CROSS

This is easily my most popular spread second only to the past present future. The spread will highlight all the key factors of an existing relationship as well as give a timeline of events in this relationship.

The querent - This represents the energy the querent is putting into the relationship.

2. The partner - This represents the energy their partner is putting into the relationship.
3. The relationships past: This card can indicate a recent past event, a cycle of behavior, or how they met.
4. Current events- This represents current obstacles in the relationship.

5. The probable future -This represents the most probable turnout of the relationship

While doing this reading it's important to remain neutral and not to be emotionally involved. It's only natural to want to see your court happy but you also must respect the feelings and Free Will of the partner. Protecting your querants feelings will not help them.

HOW TO FIND LOVE

This is a spread I offer to querants who are single and looking for love. It highlights the factors and areas that need to be developed to help bring love into their life.

1. The key issues: This represents the obstacles in your love life pertaining mostly to your emotional state.
2. Behavioral patterns: This highlights any problematic behavior on the querents part that may be keeping them from finding love.
3. Areas you need to grow: This could be behaviors or mindsets they need to grow out of or something new they need to explore.
4. Change: This represents an area that must change for the querent to find love
5. Set them free: when it comes to matters of the heart there are certain parts of ourselves, we lock up out of fear of rejection and pain. This is what you need to release.

Remind your querent that love exists inside of them and not outside of them. Failure in this area should not be made to define a person.

CAREER SPREAD

This spread is for a querent who is unhappy with their job. A bad job can be debilitating but leaving can be very intimidating. This spread helps your querent explore different options and assess their work life.

1. The current situation: This shows the querents current job.
2. Actions: This card represents necessary action to advance in your career. This is also where you will see if it is time to leave.
3. Unchangeable: There are certain factors we just cannot change. It's important to refer to this card throughout readings.
4. Current status: This represents the querents current performance.
5. Action required: This represents what you can do to improve your performance.
6. The issues: This represents what could be effecting your performance and happiness at work.
7. The reachable result: This will show if it's possible for you to move up or if it's better to move on.

MONEY SPREAD

This reading is good for those who enjoy their job but have a terrible relationship with money. This spread highlights the factors leading into being broke.

1. Your current financial situation.
2. Your ideas - This highlights your beliefs about money. Example - feeling like you are always broke.
3. Past influences - sometimes your childhood can play a role in your relationship with money. Being raised poor may make you anxious or spend it quickly where growing up wealthy may make you impulse buy and not know the value of a dollar.
4. The lessons to learn - This represents the spiritual relationship you have with money. This shows how you work with the law of attraction.
5. The action to take - This represents the necessary actions you need to take to be in a better place financially.

DECISION MAKER

Should I or shouldn't I? This spread is good for almost any situation. This will help you look at things from all different angles.

1. The querent - This represents their energy at the time of their reading.
2. Unknown - This represents the people, places or events the querent is unaware of at the time.

3. Known - This represents the details the querent knows about and should take into consideration.
4. Action - This card encourages you to act after the known and unknown factors have been under consideration.

PERSONALITY

Personality spreads are my guilty pleasure. Even though they take forever to read, introspection is fun to me. This is not the only personality spread out there, but I believe it to be one of the most basic and great for beginners.

1. Personality - General personality and conscious mind.
2. Personality 2 - subconscious and underlying influences.
3. Sources of stability.
4. The tenacity and work ethic of the querent.
5. Long term potential.
6. Short term potential.
7. Type of personality.
8. Strong negative of personality.
9. Strong positive of personality.

I hope you enjoy these spreads and continue to practice with them on your journey.

CHAPTER 3

Tarot Decks

Now that we›ve covered different spreads it›s time to delve into different decks. Contrary to popular belief your first deck does not have to be traditional. As long as you feel connected to the art on the cards it doesn't matter if it involves themes like fairies, zombies, or tattoos. It's okay to have fun and express yourself in different ways.

I own decks with all different themes, but my favorite decks involve animals. I work closely with animal totems and have animal figures come to me whenever I meditate. Think about the symbols in your life that you resonate with. That is your first step and choosing your deck. Just follow your intuition and you will be fine.

I mentioned earlier in this book that I recommend picking up an adaptation of the rider Waite. That's because most decks follow the same structure. Once you learn the rider Waite style it's easier to learn other decks. I feel like when I got to hang up the Rider Waite it really opened my world and made me feel like I could learn anything. In this chapter I'll talk about some of my favorite decks. If you're still having trouble figuring out what you need then I'll provide more on this subject in the tips and tricks section.

The Rider Waite

The Rider Waite is one of the most popular decks in reading tarot. Over the years its strong symbolism has mystified people and have been the topic of TV shows. So many decks are adapted versions of the Rider Waite having a major and minor Arcana and a royal family court with four distinctive suits. This was my first deck that I ever bought after I felt the call. I was intimidated at first but once I took it just one card at a time, I quickly formed a relationship with the deck.

I started looking at tarot card reading as a puzzle. I could write a whole book discussing symbolism alone. My close connection with this deck is part of the reason I've included the glossary in this book. Just remember it's okay if the Rider Waite doesn't work for you.

One key issue with the Rider Waite is its reliance on gender roles. Some members of the Court even suggest hair and eye color. For example, the King of Pentacles is associated with a man with dark hair and eyes. Meanwhile the Queen of Cups represents a woman with light hair and eyes. Many people are offended by how energies are considered male and female. I personally just dislike the court energy because it's generally based on stereotypes. Energy is energy. It has no gender and can change but is never destroyed. Try not to play too much importance in physical attributes. Tarot's about the subconscious after all, you're more likely to see and feel physical attributes in your mind's eye rather than in your cards.

Most importantly take time with the rider Waite deck. There are 78 cards and there's no way you'll remember all over night.

BUTTERFLY TOTEM DECK

Butterflies are very sacred to me. I have one tattoo on my wrist to remember my son. These creatures are said to be heavenly signs from loved ones who have passed on. I was drawn to the Jensen nature of the stick. Tarot card art can sometimes be graphic with nudity, death, and violence. So sometimes I will use the butterfly deck instead of the Rider Waite if I feel it will make my querent more comfortable. I especially do this if I feel the querent is too young for the rider Waite deck (Age 17-20) or if I pick up on any religious sensibilities.

This deck is great for reading young people because butterflies are a symbol of change around the globe. Young people especially in the ages between 17 and 20 change rapidly over the years both mentally and physically. That's why butterflies are such a powerful tool with young people and those dealing with grief. They help people gently work through massive changes. The butterfly tarot has Christian undertones, but they're not so bombarding in readings. No worries, these undertones can easily be omitted.

This is a great deck to try if you are trying to become more well-rounded.

ANIMAL TOTEM

The animal totem deck is one of my favorite Rider Waite adaptations because of my personal connection with animals. Many animals are revered for their symbolism like bears, wolves, and lions. However, this deck teaches us that all animals have valuable life lessons they can teach us through their way of life.

Moose teach us to dive deep into our emotions to find happiness by their surprising talent of swimming to the bottom of lakes to feed on aquatic plants. Spiders teach us to create and enjoy our life in the shadow, meanwhile mice teach us to place more value in the little things.

All these energies are powerful and give insight on what we might be overlooking as humans. This deck is easy to read if you have a handle on the Rider Waite structure then you should have no problem adapting to it.

THE WILD UNKNOWN

The Wild Unknown is similar in that its source of power comes from animals and nature. Snakes, lions, lightning, they're all there. This is a modern adaptation of the Rider Waite deck. I think it is a bit more challenging than the animal totem deck so you may need to take your time.

I will say I did pick up an instant connection with this deck. It has a potent energy that you can pick up on right off the bat. I particularly enjoy the scratchy black and white art direction coupled with the vibrant colors. I consider this deck a must-have for any tarot reader.

CRYSTALS

The Crystal Tarot is the final deck I will feature in this book. Aside from my psychic reading business I also craft some old-fashioned crystal jewelry.

As it turns out I have a huge background and crystalmancy and I specialize in knowledge of both the physical and metaphysical properties of crystals. I know which crystals are toxic, how to build grids, where they originated from, and even diagnose fake or misidentified crystals.

For this reason, selecting a crystal tarot was a no-brainer for me. The beauty of crystals helps calm people and when they own a crystal it becomes a symbol of their intents and wishes. Crystals are not a cure for all problems especially, but symbols have a powerful effect on the brain and subconscious. They can keep them focused on their issues with emotional pain. I normally use my crystal tarot to help find the right crystals for my work. I found this deck deeply fascinating with how it connects crystals to our subconscious.

I did not play a hand in creating any of these decks nor was I compensated to endorse them. These are opinions of my own that I decided to share only to aid in the journey of others. I hope you enjoy these decks as much as I have and would love to hear about your experiences with them

CHAPTER 4

Starting up your own tarot practice

If doing this for a living was easy everyone would be doing it. Reading everyday takes a huge toll on my well-being and energy levels. I even suffer major depressive episodes sometimes after work because of the emotional involvement in the readings. Even though I do my best to keep my personal feelings out of readings while I'm doing them I always reflect on them afterwards. Sometimes I come across topics that can hit close to home like suicide, losing a child, and even domestic violence. I'm everyone's mother. I've just always had a need to help and look out for people. When I meet a querent in a bad way it really hurts, but I'm forced to keep my feelings out of it. Even in the darkest readings any hope or wish to see my querent happy could make me only see what I want to see. That's why it's so important to be completely objective and bottle it up.

The talent I have for bottling up my emotions makes me a great psychic. But the price I pay is emotional turmoil and feeling overwhelmed. At the end of the day I'm a person just like everyone else. To be a good psychic you need to have enough empathy to understand your querent and know how to control that energy. Over time this could lead you to develop mental illness and, in my case, even worsen it. It's not healthy or normal for a person to have to do this on a regular basis. It will wear even the best psychic down. This kind of thing just comes with the job and fortunately and I recommend you decide carefully about whether you can handle this kind of thing.

So why do I read? Why would somebody subject themselves to so much more emotional turmoil? The truth is I love people. They're fascinating and every reading is like trying to solve a puzzle. It's difficult to figure out the issues in your life but it's much easier to find solutions to another person's problems. It gives me a sense of fulfillment whenever someone tells me that my reading has helped them. Sometimes the best way to help yourself is to help somebody else.

You need to treat every reading with importance and respect. For many querents it's the first time they're getting a reading and are very nervous. Sometimes readings can be a catalyst in a person's life, but that's not always a good thing. If you are a terrible reader and tell people they are going to get sick or die, you can make them live fearfully. This is why it is never okay to give self-readings. Readings are very delicate and before you go reading on the general public you should really consider reading on your friends or offering small free readings.

When should I offer free readings?

I offered free readings for years when I was trying to perfect my craft. I believe nobody should work for free but tarot is one of those businesses where you need to pay your dues. I worked for free for several years so that I could perform on a professional level. I have built up relationships with my querents over the years. With my free readings I became a person they could rely on.

Doing free readings is a great way to gain experience and confidence as a psychic. As powerful as your abilities are you don't know if you're a good reader until you do it. One of the main reasons people trust me is that it's been documented that I've been doing readings for many years. Longevity is not just an indicator of skill, but also shows that the psychic is less likely to be a fraud. Fraudulent psychics move from town to town and are never there for long. They often change names to try and escape any criminal charges. Free readings will protect you from any accusations as you build up your credibility. It may be rough, but I recommend any aspiring reader to put in a minimum of a year of free of charge

When are you ready to start charging money?

You know you are ready to charge when your querent keeps coming back for more readings. Once you see your readings are making a positive impact on our people's lives you will be able to judge when you are ready to read professionally. Nobody is right 100% of the time but a psychic should be right at least 95% of the time. After some time doing free readings, you'll develop your own style and know what works for you. In preparation for charging you should consider reading some books on tarot and divination. I have a whole collection of books in my room that I read through. Never stop trying to learn. Most importantly understand that you will never truly master the tarot.

Disclaimers and laws

Before getting your business off the ground I highly recommend you investigate your local state laws concerning psychics. Like I've mentioned before in New York there is a ban on fortune-telling. Even though it may be hard to enforce it is a Class B misdemeanor. If found guilty you will either get 90-day days in jail or must pay a $500 fine.

Fortune-telling is defined as when someone receives compensation in which they directly or indirectly receive money for claiming to be able to see the future or use other occult powers. With such a broad definition, it's surprising that people practice this in broad daylight. We can't seem to go anywhere in the city without seeing a psychic set up. The law almost feels forgotten about, but the police will sometimes organize massive busts.

I bet you're wondering how I have been working for so many years without facing any charges. There are several loopholes around this charge which is why it's so difficult to prosecute. On my website I have a disclaimer which states **that what I do is for entertainment purposes only**. It's not that I feel that my readings are cheap and just for fun. I do personally believe that my readings can help people address the issues in their life. However, people are also technically entertained by it and do come to me for fun often enough. Doing psychic readings for entertainment purposes only is completely legal. Being a psychic who defrauds someone out of hundreds of dollars to remove curses or heal is when police get involved. It's imperative to understand the difference.

In my practice I remind my querents that the future is subjective. I don't claim to have any special healing powers. My disclaimer is blatantly posted on my homepage. Before you do anything make sure you read up on your state laws to avoid any legal trouble.

Another thing you should consider is keeping a list of rules. These are the rules I have listed on my website.

1. Do not come to me for legal or medical advice
2. If you cancel a reading you will only receive a partial refund.
3. You must be 18 or older to schedule a reading.
4. I'm not responsible for anything that happens outside the reading.

These basic rules will help protect you from any legal trouble. Now that we've discussed the legal side of tarot reading, I'll go for what it takes to open a business.

Opening my business

Like I've said in previous chapters I spent years doing free readings to master my craft and build credibility.

On September 15th, 2017 I officially opened my business

after gaining a following on social media doing my daily oracle's. Being active on your platforms is very important so I try to post at least every other day. My business was mostly based online at the time.

You can't expect to hit the ground running. The first year in any business is the most difficult. I was lucky if I got three readings a week when I first started. You need to be patient and keep putting yourself out there. With time I got to the point where I was so overbooked that it was hard keeping up with my readings. To do this for a living you really have to pour your whole heart into it and be patient. The slow start can be discouraging for any psychic, but it happens to all of us.

There are several challenges you need to prepare yourself for. Tarot reading won't cause you any spiritual harm you're overworking yourself can debilitate your health and affect the quality of your readings. Tarot reading is as exhausting as any other career and it will physically and mentally drain you. This will happen to every reader eventually some ways I avoid this issue is...

1. Eating before a reading
2. Burning a white candle while I read
3. Taking a shower after I read
4. If I'm doing back to back readings, I will pace myself out.
5. Setting limits
6. Delegating tasks
7. Having someone to cut me off.

1. I MAKE SURE I eat before every reading

I normally choose something pretty light that will make me sleepy afterwards. I work a nine-to-five job in the morning so it's hard to keep my energy levels up for my evening before doing readings, so I forget to eat for most of the day. By the evening I am in desperate need of an energy boost

2. I burn a white candle as I read

White candles are cheap and easy to find. I don't use any special candles for burning just those cheap ones you will use if the power goes out. Burning a white candle will both purify and protect your working space and help you control negative energies by transmitting them into more positive ones. Sometimes I like to use birthday candles because they burn out relatively quickly and they come in an assortment of colors.

3. I take a shower after I read

Showers don't get enough credit for its healing abilities. It can be hard to shake off residual energy after reading. Feelings and energies will attach to you and you can carry it for days without realizing it. Water is a cleansing element and represents emotions. While I'm showering, I just envisioned all the bad running off of my body.

4. I place out my back to back readings

It doesn't matter how busy I get; I always give myself a rest period to refresh. It's not uncommon for me to have readings all night and some readings end up running longer than I intended. In this situation I need to put myself first and make sure I'm well enough for the subsequent readings. If I let myself get too exhausted, I won't be able to do a good reading anyways. I like to make sure I'm giving every reading the attention and effort deserves.

5. I set time limits

My readings are usually only set for 30 minutes. This makes sure that I don't mess up my bookings. Some readings can drag on it sometimes I'll extend for an hour. However, I never do a single reading for more than that. It's not healthy for me or my cards.

6. Delegate jobs

Personally, I find social media exhausting and it's difficult to stay on top of it and to answer every message. After about two years of doing everything myself I decided to take on an apprentice. It gives her an opportunity to work in this field, build herself up and get paid for it. She's probably editing this page right now with a stupid grin on her face (Hi Bephie!). You can't do everything yourself and it's okay to ask for help Bephie helps me with everything from answering messages, setting appointments and the valorous task of proofreading all my content. I'm thankful for her and all her work.

7. Have someone that will tell you to slow down

It's easy to get wrapped up in your work and overdo it. That's why I rely on my fiancé to tell me to slow down. He will outright ban me from doing cards if he sees it wearing me down so much. This person doesn't have to be your significant other but should be someone who knows you well and is around you often.

Expanding and goal setting

Tomorrow is always a new journey. There's always a new deck to learn or a new book to read. You should never grow complacent and constantly try to learn about the craft. That is the only way to be truly successful in reading. I'm a goal-oriented person so I love vision boards, deadlines and to-do lists. I like to make one big goal and then break it up and smaller ones.

I hope that you'll stay on this path and not be discouraged by its hardships. This journey has enriched my life. In the next few chapters I will talk about the readings to have touched me as well as other tips and tricks.

CHAPTER 5

tips and tricks

Tarot cards are one of the most intimidating oracles to study because of how much knowledge you need going into it along with a sharp intuition. Thankfully there are hundreds of things you can do to develop your abilities. Some people learn more quickly than others and learn in different ways. Do you learn by watching someone do it? Do you learn quicker by reading? Listening to instructions, or just by doing it yourself? If a method of learning isn't working for you then try a different medium that might work better for you.

I'm personally a very quick learner. I can learn anything as long as I watch somebody else do it and I can read up on it. However, if you gave me audible instructions on how to make a peanut butter and jelly sandwich, I would get confused. That doesn't mean I'm stupid- it's just how my brain processes information. Be patient and try out different methods. Some of the tips will work for you and others just won't resonate. The most important thing is that you stay consistent. The most effective ways start with our daily habits. Once Something becomes a part of your everyday life and you will begin building a relationship with cards.

In this chapter I will go over some of my favorite ways of studying as well as some that do not work for me but help many others. I recommend you try each of these methods at least once. Remember to have fun and to take your time. Nobody becomes a Tarot Master overnight

1. Keeping a tarot journal

This is one of the first things I did as a new reader. Every day I write down my thoughts and feelings after I've done my daily readings. Most people recommend keeping a grimoire so you can keep track of your journey and serve as a depository for information. My grimoire was my best tool for writing this book because it helped me remember all the little nuances of my experience along the way.

2. Sleep with them under your pillow

This is a method that didn't really help me develop a connection to my deck, but I've only tried to do this a few times. I have several friends in the business however that do this religiously. It doesn't hurt to give it a try. If it doesn't work for you that is totally okay as long as you don't let it discourage you from trying new things. Sleeping with them under your pillow is said to help create a link to your subconscious.

3. Read books!

I have my own personal library in my room filled with books about tarot, the occult, religion, dream interpretation, and even Palmistry. If you were to open one of my books, you'll find highlighted text and little notes on my thoughts. This is a way to remind yourself to look back on this later to either archive it in one of your grimoires or to research it further and fact check.

Books can get expensive at times though so one of my favorite places to go for new reads is the library. The only issue with that is I can't highlight and scribble in them. I think being well-read is essential to psychic readings and you should find a way to read up on several different topics. Learning is the most exciting part of tarot.

4. Read self-help books

In my experience some of these books are hit or miss. However, they did help me familiarize myself with The Human Condition and prepared me for giving advice. Some of these books have great information to offer for your queries.

5. Flash cards

I make flashcards for just about everything from studying runes, to numerology and remembering details about cards. When I teach my classes one of my first assignments is to make a pack of flashcards for them to study. Try making some for yourself and using them every day!

Symbolism in Tarot and collective Consciousness

There are many symbols and religions around the world. Each region seems to have its own distinctive culture and it's hard not to focus on our differences. But what about what we have in common? And how can we relate on a basic human level?

Regardless of our background there are things we can all relate to through the human experience. Even though we have cultural differences we can all relate on our most basic and vulnerable levels. These similarities can transcend consciousness and take on symbols in dreams, meditation, and other realms of the subconscious. For example, Emotions are commonly symbolized by water.

Our anxieties will often manifest as monsters or murderers, and your insecurities may be expressed with dreams of losing hair and teeth. Universal imagery is used on the Rider Waite deck, so it's a good resource when trying to memorize your cards.

Examples:

The water on the 2 of swords is rocky – implies indecision.

The Star symbolizes hope.

The horses the knights ride on symbolize movement and messages.

Lions are symbolic of strength.

Plants and fruit symbolize riches and wealth.

It's also important to look at what the figures are doing.

Do they look happy or sad? Are they offensive or defensive? What direction are they looking in? Try putting yourself in their shoes and see what emotions come up.

Simplifying the minor arcana

The minor Arcana makes up the largest portion of the Rider Waite deck for a total of 40 cards. With over a 50% probability of drawing one of these cards it's important to understand them well. However, memorizing 40 cards can be a difficult task. Thankfully each card has several tells to help you decipher the cards intent. Below I will list some simple things to look out for to help you remember them by.

Elements

One easy way to remember the characteristics of the 4 suits is associating them with the 4 elements.

<u>Cups</u> - Cups are associated with water. Water rules emotion, psychic abilities, and relationships. I like to think of the fluidity of water as the changing of emotions. Cups often have water themes like fish and shells.

<u>Wands</u> - The Wands are associated with fire. Fire rules energy, creativity, and passion. I like to think of the burning of fire being inspirational or the saying of someone having fire in their eyes. This is easy to remember by the colors used in the artwork as well as the plant and animal symbolism such as a lion, salamanders, and sunflowers.

<u>Swords</u> - Swords are associated with air. Air rules the mind, and communication. I usually think about moving

about swiftly and clearly. The sword suit is known for being extremely blunt and it's difficult to misunderstand them.

<u>Pentacles</u> - Pentacles are associated with the Earth. Earth matters with money, the body, and everything in the material world. I like to remember this by the sturdiness of Earth and the Earth as our Physical Realm. It's also easy to think of the Pentacles as coins.

Directions

It goes without saying that it's a good idea to pay close attention to what the figure on the card is doing. But did you know it could be just as important to take note on which direction the figure is facing? Directions are a very important part of Witchcraft and are often applied to tarot cards. This could help you out intuition if you are stumped.

Characters that face left tend to be more passive, reserved, and self-focused.

Characters that face right are more active, social, and preoccupied with external matters.

Astrology

Astrology is yet another one of those sciences that honestly doesn't resonate with me, but I would like to include some Tarot signators for those who do work with astrology. Here are the basic signators for each suit.

<u>Wands</u> - Aries, Leo, Sagittarius

<u>Cups</u> - Cancer, Scorpio, Pisces

<u>Swords</u> - Gemini, Libra, Aquarius

Pentacles - Taurus, Virgo, Capricorn

Numerology

Numerology has become one of my favorite tools when doing readings. From 1 through 10 each card tells a story with various ups and downs. This is a great way to find out where you are in your story and what may be coming next.

Ace represents the beginning of a journey.

2 has a message about balance and partnership.

3 is the first major milestone or change in your journey due to your decisions, creations, and collaborations with 1 and 2.

4 represents achievement and stability. It is time to celebrate or rest but could also point to obsession with material.

5 signifies massive change and usually conflict.

6 represents success and triumph over past difficulties.

7 represents mystery, illusion, and confusion, and uncertainty.

8 represents death and rebirth. This is another turning point.

9 Represents your final obstacle between you and your goal and manifestation.

10 Represents completion of this cycle.

Colors

Understanding how colors impact the human psyche is a great way to find even further symbolism. The wildly colorful outfits may seem like some long-dead fashion trend from the Middle Ages, but the colors worn are very important to the meaning of the card.

<u>Pentacles</u> - Black, brown, and green earthy colors to represent stability and money.

<u>Wands</u> - Red, orange, and yellow. Bright energetic colors to represent passion and energy.

<u>Swords</u> - Yellow, pale blue, silver, white, and black. Light colors for clarity and black to represent the unseen.

<u>Cups</u> - Yellow blue and purple to represent intuition, communication, and happiness.

Using Crystal's in tarot

As a crystalmancer, using crystals is one of my favorite things to do. There are four essential crystals I use for tarot reading.

1. Clear Quartz:

I like to use Clear quartz to help cleanse myself before and after readings. Clear quartz is basically an all-purpose Crystal that can be used for almost anything.

2. Rose quartz:

Rose quartz is a crystal I regularly give to my querents because of its gentle electrical pulse. I make sure I give it out if my querents experience tons of emotional pain during my reading to help their heart heal.

3. Black tourmaline:

Black tourmaline is a great crystal to use after you have finished your reading and need to become grounded. You can even keep peace with your deck to help keep surrounding energies from contaminating them.

4. Amethyst

Not only is amethyst beautiful but it's metaphysical properties can boost your psychic abilities as well as help heal emotional issues that come with reading. I'm a recovering alcoholic and pill head and amethyst is one of my tools for staying sober.

These are not the only crystals you can use. Sometimes I even find myself using elaborate Crystal grids during my readings. These four just happen to be the ones I use most often and are easily accessible. Perhaps in the future I will write a book about Crystalmancy!

Cleansing your deck

Some people believe you should cleanse your deck after every reading. Some people never cleanse their deck at all. Personally, I only cleanse my deck when my intuition tells me to. I'm very sensitive to energies and I can usually tell when it's time to cleanse. When I pick up my deck my head will feel static. That's really the only way to describe it. I can just feel that energy signature is off. It's basic physics that energy cannot be destroyed and that everything is energy.

Residual energies will cling onto objects. It's important to understand that you cannot destroy negative energy; you can only change, absorb, or banish it. To cleanse my deck, I will either power shuffle with clear quartz or I will break out some white sage and smudge them.

However sometimes it won't be your decks fault things feel wrong. If you are over reading, then it may just be time to give yourself a break.

Other tricks

These are a few tricks I picked up to quickly answer questions...

1. **For a situation that isn't going your way:** Shuffle your deck and sift through to find the Wheel of Fortune. The two cards on either side or the solution to the problem.
2. **To bring money to you:** Pull out the first, 5th, 10th, 20th, and 50th card in your deck.
3. **Define the root of romantic conflict:** Find the lovers. The card that either sides are the solution and the issue.
4. **To leave sadness behind:** Find The Moon and The Sun. The cards in between are steps you need to make to better your situation.

I hope these tips help you along in your journey and you enjoy trying them out. Never give up in the pursuit of knowledge!

CHAPTER 6

Stories

Over the years of reading I have many strange and interesting stories to tell. Being a psychic is probably the weirdest profession out there. People have been telling me for years that I need to write a memoir of all my crazy escapades. Maybe one day I will but for now I'll share just a few stories so you can get a feel for just how crazy the psychic life can be. But first...

For the sake of privacy concerns, I will be changing the names of the querents involved. Maintaining confidentiality and protecting the privacy of your querents. You should never confirm or deny if you have done a reading for an individual. If you are ever asked, "Hey did so and so come to you for a reading?" say nothing. To get a better idea of why you should never give information regarding querents. I will begin with a story for my inbox on my Facebook page.

I have a Facebook page where anyone can message me to book a reading or simply ask questions. This is how I ended up accidentally entangled in the marital problems of someone who we'll just call Guy. To be honest I don't even remember his real name because of how fleeting the experience was. I believe he only asked how much I charged but the conversation was over as soon as it began.

A few weeks later I'm minding my own business when a woman messages me who we'll lovingly call Crazy. I was barraged by a slew of messages with a block of text from crazy asking if I was talking to her husband. She was insinuating that we were flirting with each other because she had allegedly caught him cheating before by going through his messages.

My page is a business page and I have a reputation for being blunt. So, I tried to quell the Crazy by telling her "Ma'am this is a business account and I have no idea who your husband even is anyway." Super crazy didn't like that. "Well I looked in his inbox and I saw that he messaged you. I know you know Guy." she said. Maybe it was an easy mistake to make. I am a pretty girl so that must mean that I'm out to steal everyone's husband, right?

She demanded to know if he had a reading done and what it was about. I never ended up doing a reading for him, but I couldn't tell her that. I couldn't just say no because if I did then everyone would know that I can't say and not actually means yes. It could also make your querent feel like they were made out to be a liar. I felt like I was tied to the railroad tracks while I was just helplessly watching the crazy train speed towards me. My mother always taught me that you don't argue with stupid and you don't fight with crazy and I had a double header on my hands.

So, I told her I couldn't disclose anything and that she should just talk to her husband. I personally don't care if people know I do psychic readings, but other people feel weird about it and want to keep it a secret. It's not a good idea to give out details pertaining to someone's reading because it can reveal sensitive issues in their life, and everybody deserves their privacy. People don't only go to psychics for fun. They go when they are feeling most vulnerable and desperately need help. Every person has a right to privacy and a psychic needs to be trusted with that. This is something super crazy did not understand.

"How dare you! I'm his wife! I have a right to know you have no right to tell me not to go through his inbox. blah blah blah" Which was followed by a sequence of derogatory words that I'm not trashy enough to print.

I was never so happy to tell someone the f*** off and pound sand in my life. Even though I get subjected to a ton of crap every day at least I'm the boss. You need to treat yourself with respect. Don't be that psychic that enables crazy. This isn't the first time I received those demands and it certainly won't be the last.

Anytime you have someone come to you for love reading you run the risk of their crazy ex or significant other trying to get information from you so be vigilant and consistent with your policies.

My first botched reading

I remember my first tarot card reading like it was yesterday. It's been a source of amusement for years. I can't stress enough how important it is to write everything down so you can look back on it correctly. I mentioned my first reading in a previous chapter, but I don't think I captured the ridiculosity the first time around. I didn't even bother looking through the Rider Waite deck because I was an impatient teenager. I cleared off my table and laid down this elaborate mat that came with the deck. If you held a gun to my head, I wouldn't be able to come up with a good reason why I decided to read tarot. I was random and impulsive when I was 17. I also couldn't tell you why I decided it was a good idea to completely ignore the book that came with the deck.

What happened was a complete abortion of a reading. The spread I laid down didn't last very long. The second I laid it down my cat decided it was now her domain and that she was going to lay all over them and knock them on the floor like the little asshole that she is. This happens every time I tried to use it until I just gave up. This is also why I don't use altar cloths. It has nothing to do with energy or my reading styles. My cats are just assholes. But they are always invited to observe my tarot readings because cats love things like that. The more you push your cat away from your cards the more relentless their curiosity will become. Onix now just lays next to my readings since her curiosity has waned.

So, I was still trying to find organized way of reading was a complete abortion. I ended up just laying all my cards across the table instead of one spread. I'm guessing my cat is overstimulated by the mess because she just watched from the couch. I decided to try to use my senses to pick the right card. For a while I did this for every reading, I did on myself. Even though I don't read like this anymore and it ended up being a massive bust I think it was important because it helped me know what style I was looking for. Some people want their hand held and directed in their learning experience, but Tarot just isn't one of those practices. Every failure is a lesson and you need to embrace it. The key is to not take yourself so seriously and have realistic expectations.

The belly button story

This is easily my most popular story that people seem to always want to hear about again and again. When I say I can do a reading on anything I mean absolutely anything. However, that doesn't mean I'm willing to do everything. There are times when people ask me to do a reading for something, they can figure out themselves. It's not because I don't know how to do it but I'm trying to be courteous and keep people from wasting their money.

Why on earth would anyone pay for a reading and just ask if they should buy some body jewelry? The thing is I don't need to know anything about my querent to do a reading. Birthday, age, gender; all these factors are completely useless to me. So, when someone messages me from a functional Anonymous account I don't question it and will accept a booking from them.

I had a query from someone on Twitter from what I can only assume was a burner account. It was new, little activity, and all about belly buttons. For the sake of privacy, we will just call him Mr. Button.

Mr. Button asked me how much I charged for readings and sent me $10 immediately after I responded. Having nothing better to do now I immediately initiated the reading. "So, what kind of reading do you need?" I asked. With absolutely no delay he responded.

"I want to know if I should get my bellybutton pierced."

My heart sunk. Business was really slow at that point,

but I knew I had to refund him. Who the hell does this? Was it a joke? Regardless I had to try my best to maintain professionalism.

"You don't need to pay me to do this. If that's what you like you should just get it."

In all my years of reading up to this point I was not expecting what came next.

"No. I want this reading. I need it badly." He said. I couldn't help but laugh. There was a sense of urgency behind the message and who was I to turn someone away? It's not like I was stringing him along or anything. This is clearly something he wanted for reasons of his own and I'm not someone that should be judging.

"All right, fine. Just give me a few minutes to figure out how to do this." I said. What the hell did I just get myself into?! Using my pendulum was my first instinct. Pendulums are better for yes or no questions because the responses are straightforward. Like we explored in chapter 3 Tarot can be used for yes or no questions, but because of its vague nature it may be difficult to interpret and raise more questions than answers.

So I offered to give him a discounted pendulum reading so that he could save money and have his question answered. He wasn't buying it.

"No! I want a tarot reading!!" He said. Even with such a ridiculous request it's important to always comply with your querents request. Pendulums may not have resonated with him in the same way tarot cards did.

"Okay just give me another minute." What the hell was I going to do?! I'm not used to such a simple request. Tarot reading is never this superficial god dammit! That's when I got the idea of how I was going to pull this off.

I knew it had to be a basic small spread, so I went with my favorite three-card spread the world! I went with this spread because of how straightforward it was and how easy it is to channel into.

So, I power shuffled the deck and pulled the cards. Looks like his higher self-agreed with me and told him to go with it. As much as I didn't want to, I asked him if he needed anything else and somehow things managed to get weirder.

"I want you to tell me to get a belly button ring. Demand it." He said. This just confirmed the hidden perverted nature of the reading I suspected in the very beginning. I would need to take a shower or two after this reading because I felt grimy just from talking to him. I told him the cards demanded him to get a belly button piercing and signed off.

You're a psychic woman you will undoubtedly deal with perverts especially if you conduct business online. I have even had men propose marriage to me even though it's obvious that I'm already spoken for. In this case I have a blatant disclaimer on my page which is not difficult to understand:

"If you threaten me or act in a perverted or disrespectful manner, I withhold the right to withdraw from the reading and you will not receive a refund."

It may seem stingy, but I do it to protect myself as well as my business. Nobody should be forced to put up with that behavior and you should be able to cancel reading at any time if you feel threatened.

The suicide investigation

For this story I am changing both names and locations to protect the privacy of the family. In my first year in business I had an urgent request from an older woman who we will call Mary. Mary wanted a reading to try and get information on her son who had killed himself several years earlier. We will just call him Joe. She wanted to know if Joe was okay and if he was in heaven. Suicide is a topic that hits really close to home for me because I am a suicide Survivor myself and still in recovery. Mary lived an hour away in the city.

I denied her request for a tarot reading but told her I was willing to travel to her as a medium and see if I could get in touch with him. She was really excited, and we organized when I would be making my trip. I know there's a million reasons I shouldn't have done this especially in hindsight, but you will have times where you feel compelled to help someone. If you feel in your heart of hearts that this person needs your help it's okay to do so free of charge. I don't like to charge for my medium readings because I understand how painful grief can be. But it's a service I now offer very selectively for this reason and I don't necessarily advertise it.

Being a medium is truly a gift, but it can be really difficult. It's not only taxing on your physical body but on your mental health as well. I don't really have the best track record with mental health as you already know so therefore I rarely perform any kind of deliberate contact.

I needed to help Mary though. I felt it was important in my gut to try and help. I can't tell you for sure what exactly happens when we die or if heaven or hell exist. I have a couple of things I suspect because of my research and experiences, however. In my experience with spirits, they can remain earthbound for several reasons. Some people won't move on out of loyalty to their home or family. Others may feel guilt or fear judgment for something they have done in their life. I think when people die of suicide or in a sudden or violent manner they may not realize they're dead or feel confused on how to move on. These ghosts are not out to harm anyone but their inability to move on is likely painful.

Spirits and ghosts are classified as two separate entities and it's important to understand this difference before performing any necromancy. Spirits are souls who have crossed over and have the freedom to move back and forth freely for visitations. These entities look healthy, happy, and come with messages and do not typically haunt over a long period of time. Spirits are more likely to communicate coherently and intelligently (answering questions, responding, messages, etc).

Classifying a ghost is a bit more complicated. First you need to figure out if a haunting is intelligent or not. With an intelligent ghost they will interact with you and react to changes in the environment. It will answer questions or give warnings and EVPs. These entities are rare to come by in paranormal investigations but are a goldmine for evidence. Intelligence shows that a ghost is sentient and that the soul is present and unable or unwilling to move on. This can contribute to psychic attacks, cold spots, or spiritual retaliation. Unfortunately, parapsychology lacks a mass depository for collected information through experiments so these characteristics may vary. However, If they have even just one of these attributes they can be classified an intelligent ghost or even a poltergeist.

Ghost and poltergeists are the same thing, except that Poltergeists are essentially ghosts on steroids. They have enough energy to move physical objects. It takes an immense amount of energy to manifest and communicate and it takes even more for a spirit to interact with the physical world. If cabinets are opening, you are being touched, or things are floating - you have a poltergeist on your hands.

A haunting that is not intelligent will not interact with the investigation but will live out a repetitive cycle. This is called a residual haunting. This means that a soul is not present, and that residual energy is causing a change to the environment. We all leave behind energy everywhere we go. If you were to place your hand on a wall, then leave the room for 10 minutes and come back with night vision goggles you will still see your handprint on the wall. We all leave behind heat and energy signatures everywhere we go. Imagine the possibility that a more dramatic repetitive action could have a long-term impact on the environment. Is it possible that a family who suffered years of tragedy could leave behind a home filled with sorrowful residual energy?

It's also important to account for the physical qualities of the place you are investigating.

Quartz and Limestone famously have qualities that can store energy and memory. Therefore they are used in creating cameras, microphones, Memory cards, and even our cell phones. Many old buildings are built with Quartz and limestone. Nearby rivers and bodies of water can add even more of an electrical charge. These factors are believed to play a key role in residual hauntings by paranormal investigators.

If we can figure that we give off energy that can affect the environment, is it too much of a stretch to suspect certain memories can be absorbed and repeated like a tape recorder. Once again, paranormal sciences lack a mass depository of knowledge and consistent results unlike other sciences. Therefore, it is not taken seriously. Sadly, many groups don't realize the importance of consistency in investigations. Weather, temperature, and even moon phases should always be recorded but they rarely are.

The Birdcage in Tombstone, Arizona is a great example of residual haunting. It was the host of several poker games in the 19th century that could run emotions high. It said that you can still hear a poker game going on. Men speaking, card shuffling, and even gunshots. As a medium there is nothing urgent that needs to be cleared here because no one is in spiritual danger. I believe it to be just information stored in the limestone walls of the theatre.

I'm sorry that I had to ramble at length about different theories but as a medium it's important to understand as much as possible about the physical and metaphysical properties of where you work. You need to be able to figure out if there is any paranormal activity present and be able to diagnose the haunting.

Most of my reports unfortunately are a product of Hysteria rather than anything legitimately paranormal. I get messages about lights and TV flickering which may be electrical problems. Flashes of light which are normally just static that's been built up in the environment. Don't forget the yelling and voices that surprisingly ended up just being some foxes that hid under the porch. Make sure you aren't rushing to conclusions when there's something you can't initially explain. More often than not there is a more practical explanation for the disturbance. It's important that you have a healthy sense of skepticism with every case you work.

Over my years of psychic reading and paranormal investigation I became highly trained in recognizing different hauntings. I can normally sense it right away especially when dealing with ghosts. I'm like a bloodhound when it comes to trauma. Trauma is normally one of the first things I can pick up off a person.

So I took a ride out to Mary to start the investigation. We sat down and discussed her son Joe and the issues that led up to his suicide. Sitting there I felt warmth that was almost therapeutic. I could tell that it wasn't coming from Mary though. I asked her if it was okay if I went up to his room and she seemed almost embarrassed.

"It hadn't changed much since he passed." She told me sitting there almost like a brick wall. I can tell the rigid personality I was seeing was only to contain the emotional storm underneath and was not consistent with her real personality. She seemed reluctant but got up and started to walk me up the stairs. That's when I began to feel the pressure change. The comfort and warmth left me, and I started feeling out of breath. I'll admit, I'm a fat ass with a busted knee but even I can get up a flight of stairs without that much labor. I knew I was in trouble.

Mary refused to go in the room and stayed in the hallway. "You can stay as long as you want to but take it easy, don't overdo yourself" she told me coldly.

I felt terrible and I was immediately starting to regret coming here. In the room I felt like I was going to die. My diaphragm felt like a cinder block. I had to sit down on the bed, or I thought I would pass out right there. To Mary's credit the room was preserved well and wasn't dusty or dirty. I looked around the room at his bare walls which I thought was odd for a teenage boy. His shoes laid on the floor next to one of those old box TVs. I almost felt like I was in a time capsule.

I began feeling a deep feeling of regret and racing thoughts. I couldn't seem to focus on anything, and I couldn't make sense of my thoughts whatsoever. I thought I was going to go crazy. My perception didn't seem to slow down until I investigated the closet and it was not the relief I was wanting. The closet felt like I could just suck you right in like it was a black hole of agony. It made me nauseous. I couldn't take it anymore and had to leave.

Once we got back downstairs Mary made me some coffee and we talked about what I had experienced in the room.

"I still feel responsible for him, that's why I still tidy up there from time to time. I feel like he's still there. It's like he can come home at any moment." Mary said. I noticed her eyelids getting heavy. This poor woman is trying so hard not to cry. The warmth returned. It was probably the coffee and I once again felt drawn to the bed. I definitely felt Joe's energy, but it didn't have the same heaviness as the room did. I felt like there was something to find but what could be found after 17 years?

Against my better judgement I made the climb up to Joe's room after my coffee. The heavy atmosphere threatened to overwhelm me again but this time I felt lighter-as if there was a presence beside me.

I picked up the mattress to see if I can find anything. I felt like I was looking for a picture. I looked under the bed and in between every crack but it was no use. I couldn't find anything. I felt an increased sense of urgency to find it. After moving everything around like a lunatic I finally saw a corner of a Polaroid. Dust had embedded into the casing so it was difficult to see and felt like it could crumble into pieces just by touching it. But the discovery was the Breakthrough that I needed in this case. It was a picture of Joseph at about 9 or 10 years old and his father had what appeared to be a baseball game where he must have been playing. I felt more of the tension lift.

I showed Mary the Polaroid that she broke down in tears. Playing baseball was something sacred between Joe and his father and Jose's interest in baseball allegedly subsided after his father was killed after getting into a traffic accident just a few years later.

Finding this proved to me that Joe was no longer earthbound and that he did indeed crossover despite his horrible fate. I told Mary that there was no reason to worry for him anymore because this was Joe's way of saying he was reunited with his father on the other side. Mary had finally let her tears loose. The heaviness in the room was a concentration of Mary's anguish and obsession - not Joseph sorrow. Mary's grief had left a residual imprint in the room that was only escalated by the tragedy that had occurred there.

It disturbs me to think of all those years Mary had to suffer alone. Everything I had said resonated deeply with

Mary and I guess with her maternal intuition she knew it to be true. She thanked me and invited me over for thanksgiving. I left feeling like I had done something truly great. But it was a long trip back home and things were only about to get worse for myself.

About a month later Mary messaged me with a progress report. She thanked me for helping her and even told me she had donated some of Joe's things to Goodwill. Joe's room was still preserved but she had begun seeing a man she had met at an old job and was looking forward to a new lease on life.

I wish I could say I bounced back from the reading as well, but truthfully, I didn't. In fact, I almost retired because of it. This was my first real psychic last lapse. When I got home, I bawled my eyes out and took a shower. The heaviness continued to hang on me for about 5 to 6 weeks. It's not uncommon to come home with attachments after readings. It only agitated pre-existing mental illness in my own suicide ideations which is why I have chosen to admit Joe's method of suicide from this book. I was miserable and lived in a constant haze of melancholy. I temporarily lapsed in my abilities to read and connect during this episode and I thought I would never recover from it. I never suffered from a lapse in my abilities and I feared that I would never be back to my old self. I thought I would never be able to help someone again.

Thankfully after about 3 weeks I finally saw some improvement in my abilities as they came back slowly. About a year-and-a-half later I lost my own son Ace and it picked open the scab and now I felt I could relate to Mary's sadness once more. This is a reading I still reflect on and now

I am much more cautious to throw myself into that kind of situation again.

Being a medium is not a glamorous job. In fact, it can be downright dangerous. This story doesn't necessarily involve tarot but it's one of my most valuable pieces of advice. Protect yourself, protect your energy, and be careful about what you try to fix. If you want to be a good psychic, you must understand the dangers that come with the job. You cannot avoid trauma and sadness in this field. It's not always sunshine, love, and positivity. Real psychics do our best work in the shadows.

The most important thing is having someone to hit the emergency brake for you. For me, the person is my fiancé Paulie. When I first started seeing him, I didn't dare tell him I read tarot or that I was a psychic. Why? I might be the last person you should go to for dating advice but saying "I study the occult on the first date" usually isn't a smart idea. Thankfully when I did finally come out to him, he was very accepting and didn't run away screaming. He's the one who encouraged me to start the business after he saw how hard I worked and how proficient my abilities were. He's the one who keeps me grounded for everything and before I begin a new project, I always run it past him. Make sure you employ at least one person for this responsibility.

CHAPTER 7

The Big 3

The Rider Waite deck is split into 3 parts – The Major Arcana, Royal Court, and Minor arcana. Each section represents different variables that come together in our lives.

I normally interpret the majors as universal forces we can't control. Another way of looking at it, is the personal journey of the fool as number 0, demonstrating he can fit into any part of the sequence. It's important to remember no card is inherently good or bad, and that these listed definitions are based on my own personal interpretations. Over time through your own studies these cards may take on a different meaning for you. This section is not here to design your beliefs, but to help you see these cards in different ways to develop their own style.

Majors:

I usually think of majors as the unchangeable - almost like a universal force. I believe people can always make a choice to help facilitate a positive change for themselves, but that doesn't mean we have control over everything.

For example, death is a card about sudden uncomfortable change. I like to think of this card figuratively as the death of our old selves, ways, or habits. Like death itself, this change is unavoidable. Nothing lives forever whether it be good or bad.

So, what choice do you have? Well you could either accept the change and move forward, or you could hang on and resist change – only furthering your suffering.

Listed below are the major cards and some different interpretations for each – including some of my own personal thoughts.

00: The Fool

The fool does not have a definitive spot in the major arcana. Therefore, this card can be found anywhere because it represents newness. Pulling the fool doesn't necessarily mean you are foolish, but rather have an energy. Notice the sun rising in the east and the fool walking west. This symbolizes a new day and the fool walking into the unknown.

Accompanied only by his white dog (A spiritual companion) he isn't looking where he is going and is walking precariously towards the edge of a cliff. He isn't afraid of what is to come. He is blissfully oblivious.

Sam's thoughts: This card often comes to me when I am finally able to move on from a situation. This is my soul's cry for something new. I also interpret this card as a warning to be cautious and be mindful of my actions.

1. Magician

The magician is the first card in the Major Arcana. The magician is all about making the best use of your power to obtain your goals. His position connects him to his spirituality as well as the material of the earth. On the table you see the symbol of all 4 suits. Like an alchemist he is forging all the elements to manifest his desires. He is also surrounded by plants, a symbol of success. Notice the magician's belt is actually a snake biting its tail. This is meant to correlate with the infinity symbol above his head representing healing and growth.

Sam's Thoughts: Whenever I see this card, I try not to overthink it. This has always been my deck's way of nudging me to "Just go for it". Cards with this color scheme always make me feel charged up and motivated.

2. The High Priestess

The High Priestess is the second card in the major arcana. She is both a symbol of feminine power, intuition, and in many ways represents our shadow self. Unlike the empress who enjoys attention and being in the light, The Priestess enjoys her air of mystery. She sits between a black and white column with a moon at her feet. This shows that she has a deep connection to her intuition. Light blue is a color associated with dream and meditation magic. Anytime you see this card it is a sign you should trust your intuition and pay attention to your dreams for synchronicities.

Sam's thoughts: I've noticed that this card can change meanings depending on the gender of the querent. In a woman's reading it shows she can tap into her feminine power, but in a man's reading it can represent an unattainable woman or goal. I usually pull this card in synchronicity when it's time for me to withdraw into my study. This is by no means a glamorous or superficial card. Merge with your shadow to learn more about yourself.

3. The Empress

The empress is regarded as the mother of the tarot deck. She represents luxury, fertility and getting in touch with your feminine side. The empress encourages us to pamper ourselves. Take a bath, groom yourself, buy yourself a new outfit. The empress bears a powerful energy that attracts others.

Sam's thoughts: Whenever I draw this card I think of my motherly duties. I'm the breadwinner of my little family so it makes me think of ways to take care of myself so I can be stronger for them. You can't pour from an empty cup. You can't take care of others if you're falling apart. Go take a hot bath or get your nails done. Relax!

4. The Emperor

Like the empress, the emperor is considered the father figure of the tarot. He represents yang energy and keeping your wits about you. This card is a sign you need to be more tough, calm, and collective. Now is not the time to think with your heart.

Sam's thoughts: I don't normally ask my tarot cards yes

or no questions; but when I do, this card is always there to put me in my place. I'm honestly emotionally unstable most times, but this card helps keep me in check. This is when I know I'm too wrapped up in my feelings.

5. The Hierophant

The Hierophant (otherwise known as the pope) represents a leader or a teacher. The Hierophant also resonates with spirituality and tradition. He is not only a respected figure head, but he is responsible for passing on his knowledge. Sometimes this teacher isn't obvious. Whether we have a good or bad experience with someone, everyone we meet teaches us something. Be open to this learning and be thankful for it.

Sam's Thoughts: This card has always been a sign for me to look for synchronicities and read. I read books from the library, watch YouTube videos and browse threads online until I have that "AHA"moment. Sometimes I find this in the most unlikely places. I always need to maintain my open mind . You never master the tarot or any craft and there is always something you can get better at. I will never be the Hierophant; I am a student of life.

6. The Lovers

Love is front and center when this card appears. However, don't look at this card with rose colored glasses. This card is not just about love and romance. We all have duality within us. This card is linked to the astrological sign of Gemini. As the emperor advises us to use mind over matter, the lovers tell us to follow our heart and to nurture both sides of our being.

Sam's thoughts: This card comes up a lot when I'm having trouble with my relationship. My fiancé is a Gemini and we often have opposite beliefs and behavior patterns. However that's also why we're compatible. It reminds me that neither of us are perfect nor that a relationship is about working together. It makes me question if the issue is worth the stress on my relationship, or should I ease up and focus on what's important. Where we put our focus is a huge factor in maintaining our relationships.

7. The Chariot

The chariot is the card of movement. It encourages us to move forward with our charged-up energy. You are being driven to your goal. Notice this is not free for all energy. This is more directed and controlled with a goal in mind.

Sam's thoughts: This card teaches me to evaluate my long-term goals by looking more at my short-term goals. Am I focusing enough on my future and staying my course? Or am I getting distracted by little side quests and needlessly prolonging my journey?

8. Strength

This is one of those cards you can take literally. Lions are symbolic of strength, but this one is submitting to the angel - almost as if he is being comforted. This isn't the universe offering strength but a reminder of our innate strength. Sometimes the strongest thing to do is to turn inward instead of lashing out.

Sam's thoughts: I am a Leo and this card comes to me when I'm having a depressive episode. It tells me that most of what I'm feeling only exists in my head. It screams " This too shall pass" when I'm at my hopeless point and it really helps me pick myself up. I work closely with the lion spirit totem, so they are often a source of inspiration for me.

9. The Hermit

Now is not the time for being out and about looking for help. Now it's time to turn inward to find the solutions within yourself. You are about to go on a spiritual journey illuminated only by your lamp. Have no fear of the dark around you - this is time for some productive seclusion. Sometimes we look too hard for answers from other people and rely too heavily on that. Things like love are found inside of us, not outside of us and sometimes so can knowledge.

Sam's thoughts: Whenever I draw the hermit, I know it's a sign I've been too dependent on other people. This usually indicates I need to go further into my studies and enjoy some personal time. I often start to notice. more synchronicity and clarity. Sometimes you just need to hide away and focus on yourself.

10. The Wheel of Fortune

The wheel of Fortune represents the cycle of life. No matter who you are we all go through phases. Good or bad, it will pass. This card represents the importance of rolling with the punches rather than fighting it. Moving on can either be scary or comforting. If you are afraid of the future think about what it is you are truly afraid of and how to prepare for it.

Sam's thoughts: The wheel of Fortune has always been a positive thing for me. It pushes me to look at the bigger picture. Even when things are not going well, I always have emergency preparations in order. I also look at how the bad times prepared me for the good times.

11. Justice

Whether or not Justice is a good card really depends on your actions. If you have a guilty conscience this implies the consequences for your bad karma and bad actions will come back to haunt you. If you've been fighting the good fight this card's energy favors you.

Sam's thoughts: This card makes me look at my actions objectively. Nobody thinks they're the bad guy in situations and we're all the heroes or main characters in our own stories. Sometimes our perception of good and evil is skewed by this mindset. How the brain is naturally programmed to think this way but don't be ignorant of these behaviors because they are toxic and will harm you. Make sure you have a fair sense of right and wrong.

12. The Hanged man

The hanged man is suspended and stuck upside down. He is forced to stop and look at his situation from a new angle to try and find a way out. There are times when we find ourselves at a crossroads and we need time to think about our next move. This card is often a sign that you need to let go of fears and attachments. As a crossroads suggests you can either go left or go right, but never both. This card usually represents an unavoidable situation.

Sam's thoughts: The hanged man usually comes when I'm having a lot of trouble making an immediate decision and I feel tons of hesitation. I think about my future and what kind of regrets I may have in the wake of my decision. This card reminds me to slow down and think long term about everything. The hanged man doesn't tell me "Hurry up and make a decision!!". It tells me to sit down and dissect the issue until I understand the situation and what is best for myself.

13. Death

This card is the victim of several tv tropes. We've all seen a TV show or movie where the fortune teller pulls the death card and it foreshadows a character's demise. A tarot reader should never predict literal death from this card, in fact doing so can be dangerous. This card stands for a sudden, forced, and uncomfortable change. Like death, this change is unavoidable. It's good to think of this card as the death of your old self.

Sam's thoughts: Now is the time to accept matters and

let go. For me this has always been an empowering card. Death isn't just the end it's also the beginning to a new life. I've always found myself happier with the change in the long run. The last time the Death was calling to me I ignored it for months and made myself miserable. After I finally gave let go my life opened to be much greater. I have loved the Death card ever since and it holds a special place in my heart.

14.Temperance

Temperance is a card purely about balance. The angel is evening out the two chalices. She also has one foot in land and the other submerged in water. This represents the balance we all must have within ourselves, Between emotions and materialism. This is also a sign you need to try harder to keep yourself grounded.

Sam's thoughts: This card is personally the bane of my existence. I've had a lifelong struggle with maintaining balance. Whenever I receive this card I always make a list of everything going on in my life. Then I try to trim the fat or reprioritize.

15. The Devil

The devil is another card that carries a ton of negative connotation. This is not a card to be feared but a card that should inspire introspection. The devil does not represent the literal devil. He represents a scapegoat that we use to victimize ourselves. Over time humanity has blamed wars, famine, and natural disasters on the devil. Looking at the card closely you'll notice the chains on the lovers are loose. The devil only looks like he is holding them captive. This shows that we all have the keys to our own freedom and that we should all take responsibility for our own happiness.

Sam's thoughts: This card always reminds me to go after what I desire. I am only human after all. I usually think long and hard about what's holding me back and how I can fix it.

16. The Tower

If you build castles in the sky, they may just come crashing down on you. Another card about change, it represents our protective walls crumbling forcing us out of our comfort zone. This usually predicts a sudden upheaval (symbolized by the lightning strike). Having walls can be just as hindering as they are protective. Behind walls you can never fully explore and see the good things in the world. They don't just block dangers; they block blessings as well. People become stronger when fighting adversity.

Sam's thoughts: This card to me is a stern warning about codependency. Throughout my life I've learned not to rely on anything too heavily. This card reminds me of how scrappy I might need to be to survive and not to get too comfortable.

17. The Star

If you are hoping for an outcome and you draw the star, then you have a sign to hold out hope a little bit longer. Stars are a universal symbol of hope. How many times have you looked up at the stars and thought about your life? Notice that this isn't any ordinary star. There happens to be 8 8 pointed stars in the sky. 8 is the number of reincarnations in the tarot. Death and rebirth. This card is an encouragement not to get your hopes up.

Sam's thoughts: The star often comes to me when I feel like things can't get any worse. It's important to remember this card comes after death, the devil, and the tower. This is the natural cycle of life. Something needs to be destroyed to be rebuilt.

18. The Moon

The moon represents states of confusion, powerful emotions, and intuition. Parts of the moon remain hidden until the light of the sun reveals it. What kind of things are hiding as you go through the phases of life? This is not the time to make big decisions.

Sam's thoughts: I always consider my relationship with the moon and the respective time of the cycle. I always feel like hell during new moons. When moons are full, I begin to feel full of energy. I think everyone has a different relationship with the moon and that it's telling about how we deal with our emotions. Reflect and figure out if the way you deal with them is healthy or not.

19. The Sun

The sun is revered as one of the most positive omens in the Rider Waite deck. It's a card of overall success and feeling happy. In ancient times the sun was often worshipped, and why not? It always rises and falls in the sky without fail offering warmth, safety, and health. However even the most positive card can have darker undertones. Sometimes the sun represents being blinded and getting carried away with your feelings. Even when you are enjoying a positive cycle make sure you have a backup plan if stormier skies come your way.

Sam's thoughts: I've always had a special relationship with this card that is constantly changing. It was the guiding light of my tarot journey early on as I was trying to figure out how to read. Now this card often comes when I am doing readings about my son to see how he is doing. You'll notice over time your deck likes to get cheeky, so whenever I ask about my son, I end up drawing the sun. It lets me know that he is doing well.

20. Judgement

Judgement is very much like the justice card. It represents God's judgement after the fool's journey. Whether you are religious or not it is a reminder that we all must answer for what we've done. This is a time for review.

Sam's thoughts: This card always seems to synchronize with the tower for me. It forces me to look more closely at my behavior when I'm in times of stress. It's important to remember that your emotional state is no excuse to do bad things.

21. The World

The world card marks the end of the major's suit and the end of the fool's journey. This is a card of completion. The fool has moved through each step and he is now more connected to the universe. He has reflected on his journey and is ready to start anew. This indicates your life coming full circle.

Sam's thoughts: This card comes to me when I literally feel like I have the world on my shoulders. This card encourages me to keep moving forward on to another adventure even though I'm tired. My time will come.

THE MINOR ARCANA

Each suit represents distinct areas of your life. Unlike the major arcana which represent universal forces, the minors can be seen as choices we make and other factors that are in our control. These suits are the cups, wands, swords and pentacles.

Wands: Wands represent fire, creativity, and your career. This suit usually comes with an energy that makes you feel fired up and inspired.

Cups: Cups rule the realm of relationships and speak on our social lives. Cups represent water, emotions, and our subconscious.

Swords: Swords represent air, quick movements, and

intellect. They tend to step away from heavy emotions of the previous suits and ask for more mental clarity. This tends to carry more negative connotations than the other suits, but they can be very telling as to what you really need.

Pentacles: Pentacles represent the Earth, stability and our domestic lives. This suit concerns more of your earthly matters like your home, health and money.

Each card has 4 key features you need to pay attention to when reading.

1. What is the figure doing? How do they feel? What direction are they facing? What are they wearing?
2. The color scheme.
3. The number of the card.
4. The animal symbolism and vegetation.

Cups

The cups suit is the most psychic and emotional suit the Rider Waite Deck. They are the strongest place holders in every romantic reading. Understanding the cups is important in understanding the basic ebb and flow of all relationships. This suit is also closely linked to your inner child and creativity.

Ace of cups:

In this card the hand coming from the east is offering the chalices. This represents a new relationship on the horizon. Doves represent positive Messengers of love so definitely be on the lookout for any signs. Yellow is a color of positivity and take notice of the water overflowing in the cup. That represents your emotions.

Sam's thoughts: This card came up a lot when I was pregnant and asking about my son - which I eventually named Ace! This can indicate a major transformation in your personal life.

2 of cups:

The 2 of cups is the perfect relationship card. 2s are numbers of balance and partnership. This calls attention to the give and take in your relationship being balanced. Both the figures look happy in unison and over their heads is a lion. Lions are notorious for being strong and loyal.

Sam's thoughts: This card often comes to me when I'm in trouble with my relationship. It reminds me to reexamine the way I might be unfairly treating my fiancé. This card also reminds me that we are a team and I should run to him rather than away from him when I'm in trouble.

3 of Cups

The 3 of cups show the 3 figures dancing in celebration of their reunion. This can indicate an upcoming reunion with people you have missed. The fruit on the ground shows that this is a joyous time.

Sam's thoughts: Whenever I pull this card, I know it's time to reconnect with old friends. As I've gotten older, I've learned the hard way how quickly time passes. Between work and projects, it's so easy to lose track of time. Socializing is important to your wellbeing, and sometimes it's nice to get another person's thoughts.

4 of cups

The 4 of cups begins to take on negative undertones. The 4 of cups represent us being unsatisfied in a relationship. Perhaps we're wishing for more than what we have or are just not satisfied with what we still have. The figure is so focused on what he doesn't have that he isn't noticing the new cup that is being offered to him.

Sam's thoughts: This card comes up when I'm gripping over my exes or reflecting on the parts of my love life that went sour. Not that I'm missing them, but it's more being frustrated over how I was treated. It forces me to remember the blessings I have now and I hanging on to the negativity can poison my current relationship.

5 of cups

The 5 of cups tells the same lesson about where we place our attention. The figure is now wrapped in a black cloak grieving over the three cups that have spilled before him, but he doesn't see the two that he still has behind him. This card can represent an impending breakup or a cling to an ex love.

Sam's thoughts: I found myself heartbroken many times and I make the mistake of wrapping myself up in that negativity. I tell myself negative affirmations like "You can't trust anyone" to protect myself. I focus so much on people who have hurt me that I ignore the ones who do treat me well. It's insecurity and a product of my anxiety but it's important to remember it's a toxic behavior.

6 of cups

The 6 of cups is a return to happy your feelings and happier times. The cups are holding flowers and you can see a young figure gifting a vase to a younger child. This card is associated with childhood and nostalgia. This card can indicate reconnecting with a childhood friend or even your inner child. This card also suggests being more generous to others.

Sam's thoughts: This card speaks to me about channeling the positivity of my past. I can conjure up a more positive attitude remembering the happier times and feeling thankful. However, make sure you don't get stuck in the past.

7 of cups

The cups now represent treasures and imagination. 7 is considered a number of mysteries. This might seem like a promising card at first, but it's important to look deeper at what is being offered. The most crucial detail is that all these gifts are in the clouds suggesting that they have not materialized yet. The cups are holding extravagant gifts like castles, Jewels, and a wreath, but they also have dangers like the dragon and the deception of the snake. This implies that the dangers can even lie in the fantasy world. This card can indicate that you were daydreaming too much and that you need to narrow your focus.

Sam's thoughts: Clearing my mind has always been one of the most challenging things. I always have so many pots on the fire that it's difficult to manage everything. This card always comes up when I'm overwhelmed. Sometimes you try to do too much at once that it stifles your productivity.

8 of cups

The eight of cups features the figure embarking on a journey with a sorrowful departure. It's highly likely you will decide to leave a relationship that is no longer suited for you. The moon reflects the sad emotions of the traveler but ensuring that it is about to go full and promises a feeling of clarity. This card is not something to fear. It is merely a trial of your development.

Sam's thoughts: This card reminds me of my personal power and that I am strong outside of my relationship. Always remember that good or bad nothing lasts forever, and you should always embrace the journey ahead.

9 of cups

The 9 of cups is one of the most positive cards in the entire Rider Waite deck. It's regarded as the wish card so if there is something you have been trying to manifest then this is a good indication that it's on its way. The man is sitting on his throne satisfied with the nine of cups ahead. 9 is the final stretch. You are nearing completion.

Sam's thoughts: Even though this is a blatantly positive card no card is inherently good or bad and I have certainly seen this card in negative context. Sometimes this card can indicate that you are wishing your life away and that you need to be more in touch with what is here now.

10 of cups

We finally reached the end of the cup's suit and saw the completion of a relationship. This card can indicate a future marriage and family as two figures are watching their children play. Rainbows represent balance and divinity, so this is a union that is sure to last.

Sam's thoughts: This card comes up when I'm anxious about my future. I don't worry about whether my relationship will last, rather if I'm capable of taking care of my family. You need to be able to provide more than just emotional stability. Having a family is a huge responsibility that should not be taken lightly.

Wands

Wands are easily the most energetic suit that is supposed to inspire you and make you feel charged up. Wands are associated with the element of fire and they rule over your career path. These cards can guide you through the ups and downs of your career and keep you on the path of success. Magic wands are symbolic of manifestation so now is the time to focus on achieving your goals.

Ace of wands

You are being offered a fresh beginning with tons of potential. Notice that there is a sprout on the wand that indicates a new life. This is exciting, but remember it is still just a sprout and it is fragile. This new opportunity needs to be nurtured for it to flourish.

Sam's thoughts: I draw this card often when I am brainstorming ideas for the business. It's normally an indication that I should move forward with the idea.

2 of wands

The 2 of wands is about balancing your career and personal life. It's easy to forget about taking care of yourself when you're on your own grind. But it's imperative to make sure you are taking care of yourself, so your productivity doesn't suffer.

Sam's thoughts: This is the hardest part of working for me because I tend to jump into things very quickly. Try to dip your feet in one at a time to remain more balanced in your projects.

3 of wands

The figure is perched up on a mountain looking straight out to a Faraway land. He's made his first small goal and is taking a moment to enjoy his success, but this is only the beginning. He will have to keep moving forward to reach the promised land.

Sam's thoughts: The 2 of wands is about balancing yourself out, so I've always seen the 3 of wands as a card of reassurance. Sometimes when you work hard towards a long goal and lose sight of the smaller goals. Always allow yourself to celebrate them. It doesn't matter how slow your pace is as long as you are moving forward.

4 of wands

The 4 of wands is a celebration of job security. A stable job is something we usually take for granted. This card is a promise of happy times.

Sam's thoughts: This card is normally related to family life in my personal readings. It shows that my husband and I need to be more supportive of each other's careers. That security will help ease our anxieties. This card could also indicate an upcoming party or wedding.

5 of wands

The 5 of wands is a card that represents a competition. All of the children may be fighting with their wands, but they are obviously not looking to hurt one another. This card is reassurance that you have what it takes to compete, but you must find a way to distinguish yourself from the others.

Sam's thoughts: It's important to remember that not everyone at work is your friend, but even though the other people may act underhanded it is not a reason to engage in drama. No matter what happens maintain your professionalism.

6 of wands

The 6 of wands represents yet another milestone being made. The figure is once again proud and showing off while riding on his horse. It's always okay to celebrate your accomplishments. You've worked hard for it so you own the bragging rights. Enjoy your success and keep moving forward.

Sam's thoughts: Just in case I haven't reminded you at least 10 times throughout this book - I am a Leo. So, I always love sharing my success with others. It helps me stay accountable for my work and motivates me to work harder.

7 of wands

The 7 of wands represent your next challenge. You've risen above the 5 of wands and celebrated the 6 of wands. Now it is time to accept the responsibilities that come with your new life. It may not be easy, but you have what it takes to rise above the challenge.

Sam's thoughts: This has always been the stand-your-ground card for me.

8 of wands

The 8 of wands indicates a time of change, freedom and movement. Each wand is sprouting and swiftly moving through the air. Think of this as free-flowing ideas. Things will seem to be coming more easily to you.

Sam's thoughts: This card has always implied exciting times in my career, especially when I'm testing out several ideas. I'm a very creative person so this card is very welcoming to me.

9 of wands

The 9 of wands represent self-consciousness and worries. You're going to realize that your new life is going to have new responsibilities. You need to realize that you can't worry about your life away. Nothing is truly perfect, and you need to let go of your idealism.

Sam's thoughts: This card has always told me everything will be okay and that most of my worries are only inside my mind. I sometimes remember that I brought myself to the dance, so I have what it takes to handle my new life.

10 of wands

You're in the homestretch of your endeavors and you're taking responsibility for what you have grown. The figure is now carrying his hard-earned bounty to the market to sell. You can now enjoy the windfall that is now coming to you.

Sam's thoughts: This card comes to me when I seem to be taking on too much like I have the world on my shoulders.

Swords

The swords are the suit that will brutalize you with honesty and hard truths. They cut right through the bullshit. You're going to use your head over your heart with this suit. The swords teach us how to use our intellect to cope with the hardships of life.

Ace of swords

You see a rough dark mountain range and the universe hands you a sword. This is a new adventure and you will need to be swift and courageous in your efforts and thinking. Tap into your fighting spirit so you can handle all of your opposition. Things may also be clearer to you now so take advantage of your clarity to make the best decisions.

Sam's thoughts: This is my "it's too dangerous to go alone" card. Instead of turning to my softer, more empathetic side I am referred to my instincts. There's no time to waste.

2 of swords

The figure in the 2 of swords is defensive but knows that she is blindfolded. The rough seas and the Moon indicates that the issues really lie inside her mind and the feeling of insecurity is not what is around her. It might be best to try and figure out where this feeling of insecurity comes from.

Sam's thoughts: I pull this card whenever I'm having trouble deciding and feel very anxious about it. This usually means that I need to lower my guard and that I'm making my life more difficult than it needs to be.

3 of swords

The 3 of swords represent a separation and heartbreak. You need to make a hard decision to move forward. This heartbreak may feel like the end of the world but it's what you need to do to clear your mind and energy.

Sam's thoughts: This heart has never pursued a breakup for me, but this has always been a sign that I need to quit a bad habit. Throughout my life I have trouble with addiction, so this is normally a test of strength for me.

4 of sword

The 4 of swords is a card about burnout and the need to rest. This is a time where you should consider taking a break for a few days. It's okay to be consistently on your grind, but there is nothing productive about burnout. There is no point in working if you can't give your 100%.

Sam's thoughts: I draw this card at least once a week because I'm a chronic workaholic. It's no coincidence that this is when I suffer from creative blocks. Engaging my inner child and giving myself free time helps me feel charged up and inspired again. It's okay to take breaks as long as you never give up.

5 of swords

The five of swords indicates a time to lower your arms and a theme of betrayal. You may find yourself in a conflict after your separation and subsequent. Not everyone is going to agree with your life changes but that is okay. No reason to return to your old toxic ways.

Sam's thoughts: My reaction to this card is to keep myself covered and become more self-reliant. This has been a card that's warned me about people who act nice to my face but will talk behind my back.

6 of swords

The 6 of swords is about moving on from a bad situation. This could manifest into literally moving to a new home to get away from a toxic situation. This could also mean moving on from a toxic relationship or traveling to clear your head.

Sam's thoughts: The 6 of swords is an exciting card for me because it means I'm leaving the bad things behind. I've always had wanderlust and this card has always advised me to explore to help me feel better.

7 of swords

Ever hear the expression "Sly as a fox"? This is the type of energy this card represents. Keep your back towards the grindstone because someone may be going over your work and acting in an underhanded manner. Be cautious.

Sam's thoughts: If you feel like you can't trust someone then you probably can't. Trust your gut when push comes to shove.

8 of swords

The 8 of swords is a card about playing the victim. The woman in the image is blindfolded and surrounded by swords. A quick glance makes it easy to sympathize with her. But notice the little smirk and that her feet are not tied. She has the power to leave a situation, but she enjoys the victimhood. This can be a difficult mistake to see and difficult to admit to, but it is something we all do at one time or another. Stop pretending that you are helpless or that your life is more terrible than it is.

Sam's thoughts: This is basically my deck's way of slapping me in the face telling me to wake up. I tend to think negatively and beat myself up. It's important not to be blinded by circumstances and look for positivity in life.

9 of swords

This is a card about depression and anxiety. Worrying and negative thoughts may be keeping you up at night like the figure in the card. It is important to remember that many of our anxieties and worries mostly exist inside our mind. If you are staying up at night this may be a sign you desperately need to say your peace. Mental health issues can be debilitating to your overall wellbeing. Make sure you are prioritizing it.

Sam's thoughts: Whenever I draw this card it's a calling to take my mental illness seriously. I have bipolar depression and PTSD and sometimes I make mountains out of mole hills. This also happens because I like to take on too much at once. Sometimes I just need a day off from everything and everyone to sort out my thoughts. This card also shows up when I have a lot on my mind that I need to talk about.

10 of swords

The ten of swords is gruesome but it also means the battle is over. You may be feeling pain down, but the worst is now behind you. It may manifest as a painful ending in your life, like a final break up. However, much like the death in the tarot it represents new beginnings. This is not the end, get up and brush yourself off.

Sam's thoughts: I'm a very stubborn person so this card is always telling me to stop resisting and hurting myself. Sometimes it's better to just let go and cut your losses.

Pentacles

The pentacles represent your ordinary everyday life and needs. This suit rules over both financial matters and domestic life. Being spiritual and intuitive is good and all but it's always important to have one foot in the real world to balance you. The pentacles are here to support us at the end of the day by reminding us to take care of ourselves.

Ace of pentacles

This card represents a new offering of material life such as a new home or new job. This card can also foretell some sort of opportunity that comes your way. Make sure you take it when it comes around you take it even if it isn't what you had in mind. You'd be surprised where things take you.

Sam's thoughts: This card always gives me the courage to express myself in different ways and share my ideas. As an artist and writer, I

m often caught in creative block hell because I'm questioning if what I'm doing is quality. This is a card of encouragement and shows that my new idea is a good one.

2 of pentacles

The two of pentacles calls for a need to balance or is a sign you have too much on your hands. Now is the time to see where you can trim the fat and lighten your load. Notice the rocky ocean behind the figure; a crescent moon represents the current emotional unrest. Make sure you are prioritizing the right things.

Sam's thoughts: This is yet another card that comes to me often enough. I take on too many things at once because I fear of missing out on an opportunity. Sometimes it can be hard to relax but this card shows me I am overwhelmed and need to scale back.

3 of pentacles

The story of the pentacles shows 3 architects admiring the chapel they created and going over blueprints. This card represents the first small milestone for your plans. This may require you to team up with others and review your past work.

Sam's thoughts: This card is always a welcome sight in my professional life and reminds me to accept criticism constructively. Comparing ideas with others can greatly improve your product. Just don't let your feelings get hurt.

4 of pentacles

The 4 of pentacles represent greed and the tendency to cling onto material possessions. Ironically when we're feeling greedy, we can't enjoy the full value of what we have because we're so obsessed with losing it or attaining more. This card is as an indicator you need to let go of the coins that are literally holding you down to move forward. Learn how to weigh risk vs. reward.

Sam's thoughts: I find this card in many of the relationship readings I do. This is a sign that they have their relationship in a chokehold and that they're choking their relationship to death with their jealousy and insecurity. Codependence is normal in long standing relationships but there's always a fine line between what's healthy and what's not. This can also show that someone is still in love with their ex.

5 of pentacles

The 5 of pentacles indicates a time of financial struggle and loss. In these times it's important to remember it's okay to ask for help when you really need it. Hard times don't last forever, and a helping hand can get you out of the rut.

Sam's thoughts: I draw this card whenever I'm feeling left out in the cold. It stirs up feelings of loneliness but reminds me that I have gotten through much worse under my own personal power. In these times I try to simplify my life as much as possible.

6 of pentacles

The 6 of pentacles is a card that shows the balance of give and take. You are receiving help after the setback of the 5 of pentacles. This windfall may not be instantaneous or immediately monetary. This could also mean it is your turn to give back.

Sam's thoughts: This card reminds me that I always have something to offer. What you give does not always have to be a monetary value. Giving time a smile or just being a shoulder to cry on or invaluable gifts.

7 of pentacles

This is the literal you reap what you sow card. Your seeds, good or bad will begin to sprout. If you have been spreading positivity, Positive energy will be returned to you. If you've been spreading negativity you can expect a blowback.

Sam's thoughts: This often appears as a warning for me; it's a reminder that I am responsible for my emotional output at all times especially when I'm stressed. Negative reactions will only lead to more negative outcomes.

8 of pentacles

The 8 of pentacles is not a card about fun. It's a card about diving into your work and paying close attention to detail. Expect long days and sorting things out, but at this point in your journey it is what is necessary.

Sam's thoughts: This card is the bane of my existence but it's only because I know I tend to overlook things. It forces me to sit down and take a deep breath and then grind.

9 of pentacles

The 9 of pentacles is a card that represents long term goals and enjoying the fruits of your labor. The maiden is leisurely walking around a garden of grape vines. In the tarot grapes are symbolic of riches and success. Drawing this card is a great omen for your financial life; especially for investing and retirement planning.

Sam's thoughts: This card reminds me to look over my long-term goals and make sure they are reasonable. Sometimes I stress myself out by being too ambitious.

10 of pentacles

This card represents the completion of a cycle and subsequent retirement. This may or may not call for literal retirement, but it may indicate a cease in responsibilities and the ability to share your wealth with your family. Notice the old man petting the doggies and spending time with his grandchildren? Remember that when we die, we leave our material behind. Nothing material will come with us to the other side and it is left behind for others. What kind of imprint will you be leaving behind?

Sam's thoughts: As a family woman, this is my goals card. My family is the reason why I even work so hard at all. AlI I care about is taking care of them. This card reminds me to be a good steward of my choices and think about their future. All I really care about at the end of the day is being a good mom, daughter, and sister.

Court cards

The Royal Court is the third and final part of the Rider Waite deck. Although it is not considered an arcana, their impact can change the forecast of an entire spread. Court cards can be difficult to read because they normally represent other people. There's a belief that even physical attributes of future lovers and enemies can be predicted by these cards. For example, the Queen of cups supposedly represents someone with blond hair while the King of pentacles represents a larger dark-haired man. I personally don't subscribe to this style but there are cases in which I've admittedly found this helpful.

Page of cups

The Page of cups represents your imagination and inner child. Even in adulthood it's important to play and be creative. They helped set your mind free. This could also literally represent a child with light hair and eyes.

Sam's thoughts: This card is a sign I need to stop working and play video games or watch TV. Sometimes I work so hard I lose my inspiration. Playing keeps my dreams alive and my mind working. It may not seem like the most productive thing in the world, but it keeps burn out at bay.

Knight of cups

The Knight of cups is a famous card for being an omen of a new relationship or incoming news. The knights represent messengers and the knight of cups horse is striking a proud pose as if he were a character from Jojo's bizarre adventure. When this card comes your way try to be more open and outgoing.

Sam's thoughts: I had a dream after a failed relationship that I found the Knight of cups on the ground at Jamaica Station in queens. Naturally, this dream pissed me off because I'd rather fall down the stairs at Broadway Junction than fall in love again. But a few months later I met my future husband at that very station and I've been hooked on him ever since. This card has always been a symbol of our relationship.

Queen of cups

The Queen of cups represents our psychic and intimate selves. She has a soft easy-going temperament and is full of love and hope. She can be very sensitive and appear fragile, but her kindness is not a weakness. She may appear as a woman with light hair and light eyes.

Sam's thoughts: The queen of cups is always a sign that I need to enjoy some TLC. She tells me that I need to relax and take better care of myself, especially my emotions.

King of cups

The King of cups is the master of his emotions. He respects his emotions but always keeps them under control. He knows how to use them in a productive manner. He is in perfect balance. This man is trustworthy and normally a sentimental or creative type. This man may also have light hair and light eyes.

Sam's thoughts: This card comes to me when I'm having difficulty with cycling my moods. My moods are erratic so it's important I take time to allow myself to react and work through my feelings before they become a ticking time bomb.

Page of wands

The page of wands represents a young energy that deals with feeling inspired. Children have a way of motivating themselves that you should try to tap into. This page indicates that your career will be going well, and your creativity and ideas should be moving freely.

Sam's thoughts: This card always has me feeling charged up and excited for products I'm starting. This card also tells me that it's okay to play around a little and try something more fun.

Knight of wands

The Knight of wands is racing to tell you great news for your career. The horse is running quickly so you can expect fast ascension. This card has a charge of fiery energy.

Sam's thoughts: This card represents a new adventure for me. Trying new things and going new places help me feel recharged.

Queen of wands

The Queen of wands is a card that represents loyalty, ambition, and leadership. The queen holds the sunflower representing loyalty and has her kitty companion planted right at her feet. This is the Leo of the Tarot deck and suggests you should channel your energy in taking the lead. This could be your call to start up a business and become an entrepreneur. Either way this is a great time to take a stand and control over your life.

Sam's thoughts: This is one of my favorite cards in the tarot. I always tell people it's me and my black cat Onix working. Whenever I need to feel inspiration or see if I'm making the best career decision this card will come to me. This card also came to me a lot when I was pregnant representing motherhood.

King of wands

The king of wands is another card that is great to see in a career reading. While the Queen is more ambitious and wild, a king is more reserved; he's very tactful and careful even though he has a ton of energy. He is a leader people have recognized and someone to go to for help. Notice the ouroboros on his cape and the lines on the flag. This is symbolic of strength, loyalty, and unlimited potential.

Sam's thoughts: This card usually inspires me to visualize and closely plan my business endeavors. It reminds me that I need to be dependable and follow through with my plans.

Page of swords

The page of swords is a card of high-energy and free-thinking. The page is full of new ideas and is ready to act on them. He needs to be careful not to step on anyone's toes though.

Sam's thoughts: This card is usually a warning to me about rushing into things. It also reminds me not to be too defensive. Sometimes being too defensive can keep you from hearing others out.

Knight of swords

The Knight of swords is a card about action. News will come to you that you will need to immediately act on. Now is not the time for hesitation. Race towards your goal like the horse. This is not free for all energy; this knight has a goal.

Sam's thoughts: This card usually comes up when I'm doing a ton of rushing around and it encourages me to keep going.

Queen of swords

The Queen of swords is a person who can make swift decisions with clear thinking. She makes up her mind on what she likes and dislikes very quickly and has a low tolerance for bullshit. This is a woman who has been hurt and screwed over, but she uses her pain to educate others.

Sam's thoughts: This card represents my insecurities and hardships. I'm willing to cut anyone out of my life if they appear toxic. I just don't have time for it. Sometimes this is a good quality to have but it's important not to isolate yourself.

King of swords

The King of swords represents using logic and routine. In many instances this card will tell you to use mind over matter. When this card comes your way it's important to organize your thoughts and be honest with yourself. Choose what is the best for you based on what you already have.

Sam's thoughts: This card represents the truth. Sometimes my emotions will alter my perception of reality and this card helps me cut away the bullshit.

Page of pentacles

The page of pentacles represents good financial news coming your way; most likely a reward for hard work. Don't get discouraged if you feel like you have gone unnoticed. You're deeply appreciated and supported in ways seen and unseen.

Sam's thoughts: this card reminds me to enjoy the simple things in life. It may not be a lot but it's better than nothing

Knight of pentacles

The Knight of pentacles is the standing knight. He represents stability and your domestic life with good news regarding your finances. Him and his horse are standing calmly presenting you your reward. This knight is not in a hurry. Instead he is planning his actions. He must be ready and willing to work.

Sam's thoughts: This card has always taught me that I need to be patient. Most of my long-term goals are at least a year out of reach, but not impossible or unreasonable. In this instance I must plan my short-term goals that will eventually lead to my larger one.

Queen of pentacles

The Queen of pentacles represents motherhood and creates a happy home. She takes care of everyone's domestic needs from cooking, cleaning and providing. She is also a symbol of fertility with the rabbit hopping in the lower right corner.

Sam's thoughts: This card usually tells me it's time to spend time with my family. I'm sort of the matriarch in my house and I can take care of everyone but sometimes I get distracted with all my other duties. It's important to always put family first.

King of pentacles

The King of pentacles is a card of success and financial matters. Notice the grapes on his robe, his garden, and his castles in the background. He is proud of the riches he has built. This is a great financial omen and shows you can have financial freedom.

Sam's thoughts: This card reminds me to be mindful of my spending habits. It reminds me that I need to keep that in place so I could feel more free. preparing for the future is the key to a stress-free life.

Closing

Thank you so much for reading my first book. You deserve a stiff drink, a bowl of ice cream and a pat on the ass. Don't think for a second though that you have mastered the tarot! Like I've stated a million times, Tarot was a constant learning experience. You've got to keep your mind open. I wish you all the best in your journey and hope that my writing has deepened your relationship to the craft. Love Sammy

Enjoy the little Rider Waite dictionary I included in this book. I'm hoping it will help you look at some of the cards differently and help you with your journey. Good luck!

Thank you

Writing Your Tarot Journey has been a long journey for me with 9 years of study, practice and 3 years of reading professionally. The writing process has been a minefield of blessings and setbacks. Writing a book has always been a huge personal goal for me that I thought I could never achieve. I underestimated just how much work this was being an 18 month project, but I wanted this book to be perfect for fledgling tarot readers. I wanted to write something that I wished I had when I was starting out.

I couldn't have finished it without the endless support of my fiancé Paulino who motivated me every step of the way. Thank you to my best friend Marissa Darkness who endured the punishment of reading all my rough drafts and is a talented witch and tarot reader in her own right. Thank you to my apprentice Bephie who was also exposed to several pages of my handwriting - which is an abject horror and eye sore. Perhaps one day she will emotionally recover from the frustration of reading my handwriting and anyone who survives this deserves a pat on the ass. I'd also like to thank my assistant Linda for helping me with smaller duties as I turned my attention towards this project. Finally, I would love to thank my illustrator Omi Gomez who really knocked it out of the park when he drew the book cover. He exceeded my expectations and I couldn't be happier to see my vision come to life.

Thank you to everyone who bought my book. I hope it serves you well in your own tarot journey!

Printed in the United States
By Bookmasters